TED WILLIAMS'
FISHING
"THE BIG THREE"

Tarpon

Bonefish

Atlantic Salmon

**BY TED WILLIAMS
AND JOHN UNDERWOOD**

A FIRESIDE BOOK
Published by Simon & Schuster, Inc.
New York • London • Toronto • Sydney • Tokyo

Copyright © 1982, 1988 by Ted Williams and John Underwood

All rights reserved
including the right of reproduction
in whole or in part in any form.

First FIRESIDE EDITION, 1988

Published by Simon & Schuster, Inc.
Simon & Schuster Building
Rockefeller Center
1230 Avenue of the Americas
New York, NY 10020

FIRESIDE and colophon are registered trademarks of
Simon & Schuster, Inc.

Manufactured in the United States of America

10 9 8 7 6 5 4 3 2 1

Library of Congress Cataloging in Publication Data

Underwood, John, 1934–
    Ted Williams fishing "the big three."

    "A Fireside book."
    1. Atlantic salmon fishing. 2. Tarpon fishing.
3. Bonefishing. I. Williams, Ted, 1918–
II. Title.
SH685.U53   1988   799.1'755   87-23812

ISBN 0-671-65731-3

*For John Henry Williams
and John Underwood, Jr.,
the new blood of fishing
to follow the old*

CONTENTS

It takes imagination to be a fisherman—
to envision things and captures-to-be.

—ZANE GREY

PREFACE

It has been Ted Williams' dream to one day own a large, shrimper-type boat, seventy-five feet or better, carefully appointed with gun and tackle rooms and supplied with enough of the essentials of life to accommodate a man who eats well and recreates vigorously, and then to spend the rest of his days scouring the world for the fish he has never caught and the animals he has never hunted. He read that Zane Grey owned a facsimile of such a boat—in Grey's case, a three-masted schooner. The image of Grey at the helm, accountable only to the injunctions of wind and tide, made the writer a hero of Ted's. It is unlikely he would give Zane Grey a second thought otherwise. Williams' literary tastes run to meat-and-potatoes fact and biography, and he has little use for fiction.

Whenever Williams talks of this dream voyage the considerable enthusiasm that makes him so volatile a conversationalist—he does not converse, actually; he challenges, he needles—is rekindled. "Being there is what I love. Away from people. Away from the damn telephone. I can't think of anyone who got more fun out of life than Zane Grey, traveling the world in that three-masted schooner, hunting and fishing . . ."

The dream was nurtured during the early years of his baseball career when, as an enormously electric personality who seemed always in the vortex of controversy, he came to rely on the rivers and streams of North America and the saltwater flats and channels of the Florida Keys and any number of wilderness areas for isolation and relief. The more Williams suffered the trespasses of his idolators and the examinations of his critics, the more he retreated until, in middle age, he had wittingly fashioned for himself an idyllic outdoorsman's life—fish where and for what he wanted, hunt where and when he pleased.

He never bought that shrimper boat. He has had the money to buy a dozen like it, but he has only talked about it, retouching and dabbing at the image as if it were a painting kept in the attic for private edification, yet portable enough to cart out when a gathering needed juice. I suspect that he never will buy it, that he will just go on talking about it forever, or until he is done once and for all with the first love of his life, the love that kept him twenty years a player, seduced him (kicking and screaming) out of retirement to manage the Washington Senators–Texas Rangers for four years ("What a lousy job *that* was," he says), and even now every spring brings him back to advise the young hitters of the Boston Red Sox in Florida (for a fee, of course).

The passion for hitting a baseball is still on him, the batting cage and batter's box still beguiling places. In his youth they were the wellsprings of his expression, the laboratories where he fashioned as scientific an understanding of the art of hitting as the game has ever known. But his love for the possibilities in those simple rectangles now loses ground steadily to the full-grown tugs of nature that take him so far away from the arenas where he once starred.

The intrusion of one love on the other, competing for attention, makes Ted a lively if erratic companion. Off Key Largo I have held on, our bonefishing skiff perilously rocking as he stood to demonstrate the proper way to hit a low-outside pitch: "Hell, you can't pick your nose on this pitch. . . . You gotta be quick, be quick with the bat." I have seen him leap from a circle of fishermen on the edge of the jungle in Costa Rica to heft an imaginary bat and hit towering imaginary home runs. "See that? It's an upswing, not a downswing or a level swing. They've been getting that wrong for years, the so-called batting experts." Yet when he played, he tied flies in hotel rooms late at night and dreamed of solitary vigils in far-off waters. Once a few years ago I sat with him in his manager's cubicle in Texas as he scribbled on a lineup card and lamented the coarse blend of unproved youth and failing experience that marked his struggling team. "Cripes, this is a lousy job," he said. "The absolute worst. I'd chuck it tomorrow for three days on the Miramichi."

The fits of temper, the spitting, the gesturing, that marked him for Boston fans have long faded from the composite of his image. Cleaner, more agreeable lines have emerged with time. Like many loners, it was only the rude crowds he hated—that part of being a celebrity. It really wasn't so complicated, a matter of taste, a preference for simpler things or, one might assume, a simpler century. He was not running away from something as much as he was running *to* something. Non-outdoorsmen never quite understand that.

He is, now, an expert fisherman, perhaps the most expert of our time, the way Zane Grey was considered to be in his. The unique drive that made him desire to be, in his own words, "the greatest hitter that ever lived" turned out to be transmutable: he wouldn't mind at all being called "the greatest fisherman that ever lived." His expertise is vast. He has fished black marlin in New Zealand and tiger fish on the Zambezi, and he has won international tournaments catching near-record sailfish and tarpon. No kind of tackle, no kind of river or body of water, has escaped his attention. The weight of his experience has led him, now, to certain hard-held beliefs on the subject.

Of all the fish that swim Williams believes there are three worthy of a sportsman's consistent attention: the tarpon, the bonefish, and the Atlantic salmon. He has now caught (and released, for the most part) more than 1,000 of each. He considers it the triple crown of fishing. The first two he fishes for near his home in Islamorada on the Florida Keys. For the Atlantic salmon, he spends the greater part of every summer and fall, from June to the end of October, at his camp on the Miramichi River in New Brunswick.

What follows will help explain his convictions, maybe even explain *him* a little better. Regardless, I expect the reader, whatever his ability as an angler, to find some sustenance here for his next trip out. Morsels of wisdom to bait up on. If he has not fished any of the big three, I think he might be inspired to do so. At the very least he should come to a better appreciation of the art—and for Ted Williams fishing is certainly that. Such knowledge is applicable to any fish, in any water. Moreover, I hope the reader will enjoy having defined by, well, "the greatest" that peculiar passion that fishing can arouse in a man, even if he doesn't care about greatness himself. In the foreword of a book on Zane Grey's fishing adventures, which Ted owns and keeps under watch, Ed Zern, Grey's editor, says the American Dream for such men as Grey and Williams is expressible in these terms: "If I had a million dollars, I'd *really* go fishing." Williams has been fishing.

J.U.

1

FISHING FOR TARPON

The Experience
with Ted Williams

Ted said it was about time we showed up. It was quarter past five in the morning and the sun had not yet begun its assault on the Florida Keys. By ten o'clock it would be 85 degrees, and Charley Traynor, the photographer, would have his freckles double-coated with a petroleum compound made for World War II aviators marooned at sea. Ted had bacon, a good two pounds of bacon, bubbling and spitting in twin skillets on the stove, and the coffee was hot. He was banging around the kitchen in a way that suggested a man who had learned the breaking point of porcelain and china. "All right," he said. "Get the hell out of the road."

We were standing there like children who have been awakened to strange events.

"Just sit your behinds down and stay out of the road," he said. "We're making history here. How do you like your eggs?"

There was some ponderous shuffling as the three of us who were now his subjects found seats at the large dinette table.

There was Charley the photographer and Edwin Pope, the writer from Miami, and myself, and however improbable our status as fishermen we were there to go for tarpon with Williams, an expert at it. He had invited us to an early breakfast because he said he did not trust us to find our own at that hour and he wanted to be back at the fishing spot no later than seven. He had it scouted. We had made a stab there the previous afternoon, getting activity but no fish.

Ted said his cooking would not win prizes but as a man alone after two (now three) aborted marriages he had solved some of the mysteries of steaks, chops, and chicken. "I do a pretty fair job with them," he said. "I do not make *pies*," he said, raising his eyebrows and the side of his mouth.

He had on the milk-red Bermuda shorts I have come to think of as his home uniform in Islamorada. To oblige Charley's photographic needs, he had changed from the white T-shirt with the V-neck, the top half of the uniform, to a faded red one that had a few character holes in it. He wore Sears, Roebuck tennis shoes without socks, and his copper-brown calves stuck out prominently from the legs of the Bermudas.

In 1938 when he was nineteen years old and a pitcher-outfielder in San Diego, just starting as a professional ball player, he was six foot three and weighed 143 pounds. Eventually, after he had been exposed to a major-league regimen, he got up to 200 pounds, but it was still appropriate to call him The Splinter. The *Splendid* Splinter, to be sure, for there was more to him than attenuation. For a nickname, however, his own preference was always The Kid. Occasionally in conversation he still refers to himself as The Kid. It is a pleasing, adolescent way of taking the edge off the first person singular.

The exposed calves were a giveaway to his enormous natural power. Not weight-lifters' calves, but long-muscled calves, like a tight end's. He had never appeared terribly strong in a baseball uniform, but baseball players do not audition in Bermuda shorts. The power had to be there somewhere. There were always the wrists and hands, of course. And the eyes. People used to say he could read the label of a revolving record with those eyes, but he says that was fiction. The wrists and eyes look ordinary enough. His legs give him away.

He decided that the way we wanted our eggs was soft-boiled. He brought them to the table hot and distributed them around unopened in little egg holders and was back at the stove when we began fumbling with them, trying to get inside without burning our fingers. "Will you look at that," he said, mocking us in his loud voice. "Isn't that something. *Isn't that something.* What an exhibition."

He fixed particular scorn on Edwin Pope, whose attempts must have been spectacular; I don't know because at the time I was trying desperately to be nonchalant with my own egg. "The great Edwin Pope! The great Edwin Pope can't even open an egg. Here," he said, circling the table with a knife and spoon, deftly opening all our eggs. "Isn't that funny?" he said. "Boy."

For two days Pope had been itching to tell about an episode with his son, Eddie. Told that his daddy was going fishing with Ted Williams, Eddie had said, "Gee, Ted Williams. That's great. Ted Williams! The guy who designs all that terrific fishing equipment for Sears!" Pope said he had reminded his son that Williams had also appeared in a few major-league box scores in his day. Eddie said, "Oh, does he play ball, too?"

Pope was apprehensive that Williams might think the episode a rap on his baseball skills and the historical position they deserve. The Kid always guarded that reputation zealously as he kicked and spat his way through those stormy years in Boston, baring his teeth to sportswriters and tipping his hat to no man. I had met him then, at the tail end of his career, when he had supposedly mellowed. I know now that he will never completely mellow, which is part of his appeal—it keeps you on your toes.

I had been taken by the hand by a matron at a horse show both Williams and I were attending in Miami, and she had had the temerity to approach him in his box "to say hello." A hospitable dragon, he had invited me to "sit awhile." I sat. We talked for more than two hours, but not about horses and not about baseball. We talked about fishing. I let it out that my father had been a charter-boat captain. Precious little of my father's skill had rubbed off—he had died when I was a child—but I could at least talk a good game. Ted was relentless in his inquiries and expansive in describing his own experiences. He bared only his passion for fishing. He invited me to "come fish" sometime. But now, more than ten years later, was the first chance I had had to take him up on it.

Now Pope was telling of his son's sacrilege, risking it, and Williams laughed the loudest. He has an almost limitless enthusiasm for getting the most out of a moment. Getting the most sometimes means igniting his famously combustible temper and displaying his iridescent vocabulary. If, however, he ever had the egotist's inability to laugh at himself, he surely never showed it in my presence.

"Hell, it's been years," he said to Pope. "Your boy's a new generation. Listen. *Listen.* I'm a grandfather! Isn't that something? Isn't that funny? A *grand*father."

It creeps up on you, he said. He had been a fisherman almost before he was a ball player, and he had always said that when he could no longer hit .300 he would just quit and go fishing. The trouble was he never proved he could not hit .300. His last year with the Boston Red Sox, at age forty-two, he batted .316.

Captain Jack Brothers arrived at about the same time a little black cat began to mew at the back door in response to the clatter and aroma from Williams' noisy stove. "Where the hell *you* been, Bush," Williams said to Brothers. "We're trying to make history and you're sleeping. Pour yourself some coffee."

Brothers said Ted would be pleased to know he had already eaten and was ready to go, but he took a cup anyway. More often than not Williams fishes alone. He just gets into one of his custom-made boats—then a seventeen-and-a-half-footer with 100 horses—and goes out alone and finds his own; but he also likes to patronize the guides and has firm friendships with many of them, and there were too many of us for one boat. Brothers was born in Brooklyn but had been an Islamorada fishing guide for many years. Williams had known him but had not fished with him prior to the day before.

The little cat was now calling in earnest at the back door. "Damn cat," Ted said. "I hate cats. Been trying to run him off for weeks. I've thrown things at him—geezus, I've done everything but drown him. I fired a shot over his head one night trying to scare him. He just scrunched down and watched me." He began to gather up the leftover bacon. There was enough to feed ten cats. He opened the screen door and gently fended the cat off with his foot. "Get the hell out of the road," he said. He laid the platter of bacon down on the concrete floor of the porte cochere, and the cat went to it hungrily. "No sense letting it go to waste," said The Kid.

"All right, let's go," he said. "Let's get serious. It's time to start thinking about fishing. Bear down, Bush. *Let's start bearing down.*"

Islamorada is the jewel inset of a two-mile island called Upper Matecumbe Key, sixty-eight miles south of Miami and eighty-two miles north of Key West. It advertises itself as the Sportsfishing Capital of the World. Until the word got around about the fishing it was mostly inhabited by a tribe of big-hearted, hard-headed, industrious white natives called Conchs, who years ago had infiltrated from the Bahamas after first having fled, as supporters of the Crown, the American Revolution. The early Conchs lived on grits and grunts (small panfish with lots of flavor and bones) and Key lime pie.

Henry Flagler built a railroad through to Key West in 1912. It took seven years and cost $21 million, and a hurricane passed through Islamorada in 1935 and took the railroad out to sea. Flagler sold the remains to Key West for $4 million, and later a highway was built on top of the right-of-way. The Florida Keys were thus joined by a series of bridges, and their popularity was sealed.

The Gulf Stream runs by five miles offshore to the east, a playground for sailfish, dolphin, marlin, wahoo, and kingfish. From out there the island has a lavender hue—hence "Islamorada," Spanish for "purple island." In the coral reefs and holes there are snapper, jack, barracuda, and grouper; on the flats and back on the Gulf or Florida Bay side, snook, bonefish, permit, redfish, and the champion fighter from prehistoric days, *Tarpon atlanticus,* the silver king tarpon.

Bonefish first drew Ted Williams to Islamorada years ago, and the Conchs have helped keep him there. The best thing about Conchs, Williams found, was that they did not make a fuss over him. He could fish in peace. As the years went by, he ran his box score to over a thousand bonefish. When he quit playing ball and could fish in May, he switched to tarpon as the principal quarry. He became hooked on tarpon. In 1964 he needled the Islamorada Fishing Guides Association into putting together a highly selective, invitational tarpon tournament called the Gold Cup, which he won twice. The guides say if it is not the best fishing tournament in the world, it is certainly one of the most wagered-on. The Kid was using our trip to get himself tuned up for the tournament.

Williams had left his boat from the previous day at a marina south on Long Key, where he had a standing fifty-cent bet with the proprietor that every time he went out he would get a tarpon. It would be quicker by car to Long Key, and from there quicker by boat to the spot. We piled into Williams' station wagon, and he drove.

The Kid drives much the way he used to ready himself to hit a baseball: convulsively. He sometimes finds it necessary to take both hands off the wheel to make a point in conversation. He turns around to face inquiries from the back seat. When he comes to bridges he makes short, involuntary honks of the horn to greet or to warn fisherman or to make a fisherwoman turn her head. He steers with his knees. He does not drive slowly.

To fish with Williams and emerge with your sensitivities intact is to undertake the voyage between Scylla and Charybdis. It is delicate work, but it can be done, and it can be enjoyable. It most certainly will be educational. An open boat with The Kid just does not happen to be the place for anyone with the heart of a fawn or the ears of a rabbit. Even his friends call him the Captain Queeg of fishing. There are four things to remember: one, he is a perfectionist; two, he is better at it than you are; three, he is a consummate needler; and four, he is in charge. He brings to fishing the same hard-eyed intensity, the same brooding capacity for scientific inquiry, he brought to hitting a baseball.

Fishing guides are, by reputation, bullies. They bully their clients because the fish they flop on the dock at day's end is their reputation. They cannot trust incompetence to do the job. No single group of men has insulted as many board chairmen and company presidents.

The guides do not bully Williams.

Jimmie Albright, who has guided him since the '40's and is more or less a regular companion the eight months a year Williams lives in Islamorada, says that this is because Williams knows more about fishing than they do. This from a man who can grab bare-handed a 100-pound tarpon by its angry mouth and bring it into the boat.

They share admiration for each other, Williams and Albright. Waiting at the batting cage in Boston one day years ago, Williams made the offhand remark that he might very well be the greatest fisherman in the world. When his interrogator asked who could possibly have made such a judgment, he replied, "Jimmie Albright." "Who is Jimmie Albright?" "The best damn fishing guide on the Florida Keys," said Ted, and hit a ball out of the park.

With guides and other experienced anglers Williams encourages a constant flow of ideas, theories, and critiques, of digs and approvals. His favorite appellation is "Bush," short for bush leaguer, a baseball term meaning less than major-league, but with Williams an affectionate accreditation. If he calls you Bush, you're in—and in for it.

Bush Brothers was on his guard from the first day, when we were sitting in Williams's living room mapping plans, and the subject turned to sharks. Jack casually mentioned that he had seen a great white, the dreaded man-eater, down at the Content Keys a few years before. Williams leaped out of his chair. "Impossible," he said. "You got some funny ideas, Bush," he said and pulled from a bookshelf *The Wise Encyclopedia of Fishing*. "Look here, I opened right to it," he shouted. "Isn't that funny?" And he began reading passages on the hunting grounds of the great white shark.

"Geez, Ted," whined Brothers, "a guy tells a fish story and you pull an encyclopedia on him."

That first day we had gone with the falling tide to a spot a mile east of Long Key. Most of our time there was spent situating the boat in the prospective line of the tarpon run, at the edge of a channel. Naturally, Williams questioned Brothers' choice of position. Brothers asked him if he brought his fly rod, just in case. "I think you'll find spinning gear better by two to one today," said The Kid. "I think you will also find I'm prepared, that I'm very . . . well . . . prepared."

He began to change lures, from a bucktail dyed red and yellow to one dyed pink. He makes his own lures. Brothers said that the color of the lure was to satisfy the fisherman, not the fish; that it was more a matter of "proper presentation." "Baloney," said Williams. He presented his hook for Jack to touch. A sharp hook is essential for tarpon because their mouths are rock hard. "You ever seen a sharper hook, Bush?" he said.

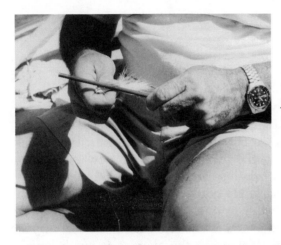

Sharp hooks are a must for tarpon. Using a thin, round file, Ted hones the hook from all sides.

His fingers moved nimbly with the line, tying the necessary knots. He bit off the ends with his teeth. He winked at me. "Boy, the guides would like to know how to tie *that* knot," he said. "That's one knot I'll never show them. A hundred-percent knot." Jack said there was no such thing as a 100-percent knot. They argued the point for a while and Brothers tied a knot of his own that Williams evaluated as a 60-percenter.

The Kid put on a shapeless white hat and an extra layer of grease on his lips and assumed his waiting stance atop a tacklebox, looking out across the water, his left hand on his hip, his right holding the weapon: a Ted Williams signature reel with fifteen-pound monofilament line and a Ted Williams seven-foot rod, both made by Sears.

From the tacklebox he could make conversation and watch for the coming of the tarpon. The practiced eye can see their shadows in the water; the casual fisherman can sometimes spot them by the ripples they push ahead as they feed or play, or the slice of their dorsal fins as they roll near the top. At his post, The Kid was a relaxed sentinel, rolling on the sides of his feet as he kibitzed with the rest of us. He gave the impression that he could stand there for hours, waiting. Brothers said he would have been just as relaxed waiting for fly balls in Boston, "but the fans in Fenway Park gave him too much hell."

Putting the bite on a knot to finish it off. Knots are the weak links of a rig. They must be tied carefully and checked often for wear.

"Bear down, Bush. Just bear down," said The Kid.

When the fish came, Ted's appearance abruptly changed. He went into a crouch, like a linebacker anticipating a ball carrier. Where before only his eyes were alert, the prospect of action now galvanized the rest of him. When he made his cast, it was quick and sure. His wrist action was extraordinary. He got three casts in before the fish passed out of range.

It is Ted's opinion that he averages one score for every five tarpon that strike. For lesser tarpon fishermen the average is much lower, about one for ten. That first day he had four fish on the line, one down at Long Key. When we switched across to the Florida Bay side, seven miles southwest of Islamorada on the edge of Buchanan Bank, catching the falling side there, he had three more.

The water around Buchanan is only three to seven feet deep in the "lakes," as the Conchs call them, that are spotted through the channels and shallows. The tarpon swing along the edge of the lakes. Though silver-black in the clearer water off Long Key, they appeared more greenish yellow here because they were passing through the mud raised by schooling mullet. On this side, especially in June, Brothers said, the tarpon tend to be especially cooperative.

The first one jumped and spit out Ted's bucktail. The second rolled and spit it out. Finally the third took it firm and exploded in the air. *Suwhack-whack-whack.* With three lightning whips of the rod Ted set the hook in an unwilling mouth. The tarpon jumped seven times, soaring spectacularly into the air as Williams played it, worked it, reeled, kept the pressure on. All the time he was instructing us, explaining what he was doing and why, advising Charley in the second boat when to shoot and what lens opening to use, cautioning Jack about getting too eager with the gaff.

22

*Using a new reel with an experimental bail, Ted caught this 130-pounder
with his first cast of the day off Islamorada several years ago. It is one
of the last tarpon he kept.*

23

*Playing a big tarpon
is a test of tackle as
well as an angling
skill and strength.
Here Ted adjusts the
drag as he plays the
fish, keeps pressure
on underneath the
butt of the rod to get
the proper bend,
and constantly works
against the swim of
the fish to tire it.
He does not try to
"lift" a tarpon, but
(facing page, top)
works his rod oppo-
site the fish's line
of flight.*

A tarpon cannot be given a moment's rest. Ted applies constant pressure against the fish's breathing system.

With a short-shank gaff, guide Jimmie Al-bright brings a tarpon in. Gaffing through the lower lip allows for a quick and relatively painless release.

"It's a medium-size fish . . . about fifty to sixty pounds. When he rolls, that's the time to put the pressure on. If you can turn him there, it takes a lot out of him. After he jumps, get on his butt again. . . . See how I lighten the drag when it's under the boat? . . . Watch, now, he'll jump when I say 'now.' Be ready to shoot. . . . *Now!*" And the fish was up again, just feet away from the boat. He applied constant pressure, keeping the pull of the line opposite the head of the fish, tiring it. Then when he had it next to the boat and Brothers stood waiting with the gaff, the glistening beast slipped the hook, as if at that critical moment it decided the episode had become distasteful, and it was gone.

I had heard of the carnage when the Williams temper stirs. The fractured golf clubs. The snapped fishing rods. The busted water coolers. He does not have much sympathy for failures in the clutch, no matter who or what is responsible. Once on this same Buchanan bank, when he was going through his paces for a movie photographer, a tarpon he was playing actually jumped in the boat. He predicted aloud that it was about to happen, gauging the line of the jump, and when he discovered the photographer had missed this wildest of scenes, he paid him off on the spot and told him to just get the hell back to shore. With himself, moreover, he is especially severe, so I expected him to blow. But he did not. "That's all right, it happens," he said calmly. "It happens."

Meanwhile I found time to make a few tentative tries myself at getting in the way of a tarpon. I had made up my mind not to attempt a fiction that I knew what I was doing. By pointing out that I had never gone for tarpon, I thus provided myself insulation against an inevitable embarrassment. Things not done out of habit usually feel awkward, and awkwardness is the mother of error.

In short order I proved that if I was no tarpon fisherman, I was also no liar. Williams began to refer to my casts as Chinese, as in Chinese home runs, or bloopers. He tried to advise me. I popped another straight up into the air. "Damn," I said. But a fish hit my line anyway. I felt the strike and saw the fish almost simultaneously. It exploded into the air right next to the boat, a massive silver blur, and broke the line. "Wow," I said.

Williams was comforting. "It wasn't your fault," he said. "It must have been one of Jack's knots." He grinned as Jack Brothers sputtered, trying to make a comeback.

Now, with the sun just rising and Charley Traynor lathering up with his World War II suntan lotion, we were heading back out to

Buchanan. "Bet you a hundred dollars I get one today," said The Kid. Over the drone of his 100 horses he and Brothers began a discussion on the amount of drag necessary for tarpon. They differed sharply. Jack preferred a heavier drag, about seven pounds; Ted said that heavy a drag would pop your line when you got a "real hot fish" and brought up my miss as an example. The argument carried on to Buchanan Bank.

Brothers got us situated, following Ted's directions. We were on the edge of a "lake," but anchored in shallow water. The angle of the sun made no shadows on the tarpon's expected line of passage, and we could see to a comfortable depth.

In the quiet moments as we waited, the sun gaining strength, Ted opened up a number of topics for discussion, sampling each one as if it were an unlabeled canned good offering new possibilities. He has an active intellectual curiosity. The things he knows and feels sure of he is adamant about—baseball, the right length for a fishing rod, the value of his time—the things he does not know he wants to know. He wants to know what *you* think, right here in the car, in the living room, in the boat. From Charley he wanted to know about cameras and about his new Thunderbird. Is there enough room in there? Listen, Edwin, tell me about So-and-so. Is he much of a fighter? What do you think about the stock market? The interest rates? The price of a rib roast?

He carted out some of his stronger notions about baseball: how it could better serve a faster generation by limiting the season to 140 games and by playing seven-inning second games in doubleheaders. He said too much leisure was keeping talented kids off the diamond, and it was a shame. He said he seldom saw a game in the flesh anymore. He said he still felt hitting a baseball took more individual talent than anything in sport, more individual work. He said he "loved Joe Cronin" but that Joe McCarthy was the greatest manager he ever played for. Most of the others, he said, were just "guys in the dugout."

It was just after eleven o'clock when the tarpon hit. Actually it hit Ted's second cast; it passed by his first, spooking slightly, and he had to put the second one out eighty feet. It jumped, exposing its great contorted body, the scales jangling like castanets. It was obviously bigger than the one he had lost the day before and close enough for me to feel the spray from its prodigious leap. Swiftly Williams joined the battle, planting the hook with those three quick whips of the rod, waiting for the proper moment to pull again against the screaming line as the tarpon fled in terror.

A tarpon strike is always explosive.

The fight is on—modern angler v. prehistoric monster.

An adept guide—here Ted's old friend Jimmy Albright— makes the crucial difference in gaffing a powerful tarpon. The trick is to do it without damaging the fish, making its release possible.

He moved with the action, leaning, sitting down, knees bent, knees straight, talking, checking the drag, getting Jack to maneuver the boat. A mixture of suntan oil and sweat got into his eyes, and he wiped at it with his left hand. We were a quarter of a mile from the spot where the tarpon hit when he got it up to the boat, and then he had to frantically pass the rod under the gunwale and grab it on the other side as the tarpon battled desperately.

"I hope it isn't this tough in the damn tournament," said Jack.

"It will be," said The Kid.

The nose of the tarpon thudded into the stern of the boat, and it moved off. Jack wanted to gaff it. "I'll tell you when I'm ready, Bush. I'm going to put him right there at the side. I'll tell you right where he'll be. Don't try to do anything unless he's ready." He yelled to the other boat where Charley Traynor was clicking off pictures. "Get closer, bring it closer so he can get this. I'll lead him right up. Careful"—Jack had the gaff poised—"don't scare him, don't scare him, all right. *All right.*" The gaff pierced the lip of the tarpon.

They hoisted the fish up in the air. "Ninety-five pounds," said Brothers. It had taken thirty-five minutes.

"A guide's dream," said Brothers. "All you do is pole the boat and gaff the fish when he says gaff it."

"Here, look at this," said Ted, displaying the wooden head of the red and yellow bucktail lure that he took from the fish's mouth. "Isn't that something? He split it in half."

They lowered the stricken tarpon into the water, and Jack began to work it around, forcing water through the gills. Gradually the big fish revived. "He's going to make it," said Ted. "He's all right, he'll make it. He'll make it unless some shark comes along and bites his ass. All right," he said, "Lunchtime."

Ted Williams' home is easy to find once you have found it the first time. It is on the west or Florida Bay side of the island, down a road that runs perpendicular to U.S. 1. Faded signs mark the intersection—Maderia and List roads—but they are not to be taken seriously. If you ask a native where Ted Williams lives, he will direct you by landmarks, not street names.

When he went to Islamorada to live he bought a house on the ocean side, but in 1960 Hurricane Donna shoved the house around, and he retreated to the lee side of the island. He has two and a half acres. The two-story, three-bedroom white stucco house backs up to a small lagoon where he has a concrete dock and the coconut trees hang over the water. The property extends 200 feet into the water. He practices casting there, aiming at a white plastic bottle bobbing 75 feet off shore. One day when I was there he was sitting with a friend, watching through binoculars out the rear window as a white crane stabbed for fish in the lagoon. He marveled at the skill with which the bird made its kill.

The front of the house is camouflaged by a grove of rubber trees and gumbo-limbo and lignum vitae and sea grapes, all hemmed in by a high chain-link fence, with a no-trespassing sign for emphasis and a burglar alarm for protection. Separated from the main house is a small shed where he keeps his large supply of fishing equipment and tools, and where he devotes hours to tinkering around and making lures. He holds one up, fresh off the workbench: "Now that's a well-tied fly. I'd buy that fly."

"Williams" is in small script on the front screen door, yet except in the den upstairs there is little on display to associate the name with baseball. The album of photographs in the living room is mostly of fishing triumphs; mounted fish hang on the walls; and two beautiful salmon flies sit suspended in glass on top of the TV set.

On the cyprus-paneled den walls are the pictures that go back. There is a skinny kid with curly hair and a Robert Ryan smile, standing at the train station in Boston in a double-breasted suit and white-tipped brown shoes. There are autographed photographs of Cardinal Cushing and Tom Yawkey. There is one of The Kid and Casey Stengel at Cooperstown and another of The Kid swinging a bat. And there are some of his prize catches: a 1,235-pound marlin he got in New Zealand; a twenty-pound salmon he got the day after he beat out teammate Pete Runnels for the American League batting championship on the last day of the 1958 season.

His celebrated appetite for privacy has not been diminished by the years. His phone number is unlisted. It is not even printed on the receiver. When it gets to be too well known, he changes it. To get in touch with him requires going through his secretary. Then *he* calls *you*. And when he says he will call at 7:30, he calls at 7:30, on the dot. Presumably, close friends and fishing guides and tennis opponents—a growing number—are the only ones who know how to make direct contact, and Conchs don't snitch. In turn he seeks out their company. Often in the mornings, at daybreak, he materializes at the Islamorada tackle shops where the guides congregate, and he hangs around, ribbing and kibitzing.

"Going out today, Ted?"

"Hell no. You're not going to catch me screwing around with that crap."

He then adds a few colorful lies about what he "really" thinks of fishing, none of which the guides take seriously. He has been especially close to Jimmie Albright. He was visiting at the Albright house when word arrived that he had been called back to the service for the Korean War in 1952. When an Associated Press reporter came around to interview him, Ted jumped into one of Albright's closets. Albright invited the reporter in and deliberately made small talk for an hour while Williams sweated quietly in the closet.

Lunchtime often finds him patronizing a small Spanish restaurant called Manny and Isa's, just on the other side of the Overseas Highway, on a crusty access road that used to be the highway. He prefers it there because recognition is less likely than elsewhere and he can wear his fishing uniform, the red Bermudas and white T-shirt, without apologies and because the food is excellent.

We ate there. Cuban sandwiches all around, recommended strongly by The Kid. He suggested beer to drink, a surprise to me. When he was younger he existed almost exclusively on milk shakes and was known for his teetotaling. He said the acceptance of alcohol by his system had come with "getting old and fat." He still bridles, however, when caught downwind of cigarette smoke.

"What are you, a chain smoker?" he said to Pope, making him change seats. "Damn."

I asked if, in view of the obvious effort he puts into fishing, he got as much satisfaction from it as he had from his baseball. Not exactly, he said, because success at baseball had required more hours of practice, more competition, more everything, but that the deeper he got into fishing, the more he realized how much there was to it. And for that matter how little many of the "experts" knew.

We went back out to Buchanan in the afternoon and fished unsuccessfully until dark. Williams brought a radio along and lay back on the deck so he could watch Jack and me in action. Having caught his fish for the day he was prepared to needle away his time. "I want to see this," he said. "I've got to see this." Before long, however, he was up with us.

At dusk the conversation got back to the merits of a tight drag, and the argument heated up again. The Kid said, "All right, Bush, I'm just trying to help you. But I'm going to prove it to you. A hot fish—a *hot* fish will break your line with that drag."

Early in his work for Sears, Williams fished for tarpon with experimental gear. This fish was landed with new spinning tackle under the eye of Jimmie Albright.

It was almost dark when we returned. "C'mon," he said to Jack. He got Jack's line and tied it around his waist, and in the semidarkness lumbered off into a ragged field of weeds and coral rock, lurching as he picked up speed over the treacherous ground. When he gave a sudden yank . . . *whack* . . . the line popped. "Isn't that funny, Bush?" he shouted. "Isn't that funny?"

The next week, with Jimmie Albright as his guide, Ted won the Gold Cup tarpon tournament for the second time. He won it on the last day of the tournament. That morning he was in eleventh place; by mid-afternoon he had caught five tarpon.

Before the tournament the betting got lively, and the two of them, Jimmy and The Kid, wound up with $1,100 riding on the outcome. Every time Jimmie ventured toward a group of anglers and guides, Ted would say, "I don't know what you have in mind, Bush, but you better bring your checkbook Friday night when this is over."

When the bets were collected, he gave the entire $1,100 to Albright, plus an extra $200 he claimed he won but Jimmie doubts. He also gave Jimmie the gold tiepin with the leaping tarpon that went to the winner. The Kid does not wear ties.

Jimmie said every morning before they went out during the week of the tournament, Ted stopped to feed the little black cat. "The cat was so darned determined," said Albright. "He just kept hanging in there. And Ted hates cats, you know."

A few weeks later I had occasion to be back at Islamorada, and Brothers took me out to Buchanan for an afternoon. Ted had already left for his fishing camp in New Brunswick, and in relative privacy, with Jack to instruct me, I worked on lengthening my casts and got so I could put it out there with at least bush-leaguer authority.

Late in the afternoon I had my second strike, and the hook went deep, and the tarpon burst into the air. Right away Brothers and a guide in a nearby boat estimated the fish at 120 to 130 pounds, a big tarpon. It dragged us all over the bay, draining the strength from my arms, but after forty-five minutes it was by the boat, winded and on its side. Brothers applied the gaff, aiming for the belly, but he was slightly off. The gaff dug into the monster's glistening side, tearing flesh and a half dozen large scales. The act provoked a last violent thrash. The tarpon's tail came across and severed the line.

I sent a handful of the scales to Ted at his camp, with a note of exaggeration. I blamed the loss on Jack Brothers's knots. The Kid wrote back a few days later and said he was glad I gave my guide hell. "He deserved it," he wrote. Then he inked in over that, "Not really."

The Expertise:
Ted Williams on Tarpon

The Fish—and Where to Catch It

A dynamic, eager, tackle-busting—well, just a sensational, spectacular fish. For excitement in angling there's nothing like a tarpon. For gameness it's better than any of them—it jumps better; it tests your ability to handle tackle better; it takes any kind of lure, artificial or live. And to make the joy complete, the contest is almost always set at close quarters, using what is basically freshwater equipment. That means fairly light line, without the best drags or the fastest retrieves.

For tarpon, therefore, your line has to be just right, your knots have to be just right. Everything has to be right, including your nerves, because taking on a fighting machine that's liable to be almost as big as you are, that's leaping around so close you think he's going to jump in the boat—which has happened to a lot of anglers, including me—is not a thrill you'd want to have cut short. Literally.

That first time a 125-pound silver rocket goes off twenty feet from your skiff, gills jangling, water flying, you'll know what brought you to tarpon fishing. There is nothing like it—a big-game fish in a small-tackle environment. And every time it happens thereafter, it will take your breath away.

The tarpon is a carry over, a prehistoric fish (*Tarpon atlanticus;* also known as *Megalops atlantica*). They still don't know much about its origins, which might be why it has stayed around so long, that and the fact that it is about as edible as an old shoe, but it is supposed to be related to the herring, which is something you won't believe when you've been fighting one.

They range up and down the Atlantic Ocean, from Brazil as far north as Cape Hatteras. They are incredibly adaptable and can be found in almost any kind of water in those areas—in the ocean, the gulf, in brackish bays and passes, in freshwater canals.

Tarpon studies were very late getting underway and are still in-

37

complete, but everything indicates they spawn at sea, the female dropping as many as twelve million eggs at a time, and the males coming along to fertilize them as they migrate north in the summer. The larval tarpon stay out, but when they become young fish they are carried into the shoreline areas, into the inlets and canals and into the bays. Some never go back.

I've fished for them in all the places where they are most abundant and where the biggest have been caught—along the Gulf of Mexico in Central America and Texas, on both sides of the lower Florida coast, in the Bahamas, and in the West Indies. Tarpon as large as eight feet and 300 pounds have been netted. A guy in Venezuela got one on thirty-pound trolling tackle that weighed 283 pounds. The biggest one caught around the Florida Keys was a 243-pounder, on twenty-pound line in the Key West harbor. Of the more than 1,000 I've caught, I'd estimate 200 to 250 were more than 50 pounds, and there seemed to be a definite correlation between their size and where they were in the migratory pattern.

You could practically walk across the rolling tarpon at the mouth of the Parismina River in Costa Rica when I fished there. But they weren't as big as they get in the Florida Keys, both on the Florida Bay side and the Atlantic side, indicating a lesser maturity. Consistently, I've seen even bigger ones at Boca Grande and Homosassa Springs on the Florida west coast, and they were much tougher fighters. But don't be misled—*all* tarpon fight.

My first choices for spots would be around Islamorada south to Key West on the Florida Keys, at Homosassa Springs north of Tampa, and for sheer numbers around Boca Grande just north of Fort Myers. There are many more miles of fruitful tarpon water in the Keys, but the Homosassa area will consistently produce larger fish—and many stories about the 200-pounders that got away. Al Pfleuger, a great angler, is among those who believe the tarpon of Homosassa are from different parentage because they have thicker bodies, more girth per inch. It could be, however, that they are just an advanced step up the migratory ladder. No one knows for sure.

As I said, there is great variety to tarpon fishing, and no matter where or how you go about it there is bound to be excitement. But my interest is sight fishing—true angling with precise equipment. I have no interest in some of the ways and places tarpon are fished, although it's probably true that more are caught from charter boats drifting or trolling with live bait in deeper water, twenty to sixty feet, than any other method.

In Boca Grande pass the big boats drift with thirty- to fifty-pound test line on trolling rods and baited with live pinfish, squirrel fish, and crabs, and they catch a lot of tarpon. Around the Bahia Honda bridge on the Keys charter boats fish in fifteen to thirty feet of water with live mullet. I don't doubt the customers have fun, but 90 percent of the skill is the boat captain's. The angler is fishing blind.

Contrast that with plug casting or spin casting in shallow water from a seventeen-foot open boat. Searching the fish out, catching it. Or, best of all, fly-fishing under the same circumstances. Since Jimmie Albright took Gerry Coughlan out in the 1950's and proved conclusively you could take 100-pound tarpon on light casting equipment, I've grown steadily in my belief that fly-fishing and heavy spinning and casting are the ways to go for the complete tarpon experience.

This book is more for the angler who stalks his prey, which for me is half the enjoyment and maybe at least that much of the skill. Once you get into tarpon, you won't believe how much fun it can be just finding the fish.

In places you know are tarpon hot spots, look for an inlet with flats around it or along the edges of channels near islands. A depth of five to eight feet and a white bottom is preferred so you can see the fish moving. A favorite of mine is a place on the Atlantic side of Indian Key near Islamorada where there is a white-bottom flat between two channels working in from the ocean. You can see the tarpon coming a good 100 yards away there, even if they're not rolling.

Tarpon have a tendency to patrol with the tide near the edges of flats, foraging for food, then take the channels out as the tide drops. They advance or retreat to and from larger bodies of water—bays, the gulf, the ocean. They make their way along the edges as they go. In Florida Bay you look for a basin or a lake coming up to the lip of a shallow bank. In Costa Rica the hot spot was inside the mouth of the Parismina River, 200 yards from the boiling Caribbean Sea, but they were just as plentiful back in the lagoons, where there was a confluence of tributaries.

Your best bet for finding them—*always* for those first times out—is to hire a guide who knows the area and knows the fish. Learn the ropes by buying a little experience. I seldom go a season in Islamorada without engaging Jimmie Albright for a few trips. I always learn something—about the fish, about the places to find them. Nobody in the world knows more about tarpon than Jimmie Albright, and it's an education to be with him even for a day, and even if we don't always agree.

*Fly casting for tarpon with heavy equipment on a sun-
scorched day does not make for the most formful fishing. But the object of a cast is to get the fly to the fish,
and Ted drives this one out. The homemade basket on
his hip holds stripped line so that it won't tangle in
the boat; the hat and handkerchief protect against the
elements.*

The Tackle

If there is one thing I am an absolute nut about in fishing, it's adequate tackle—the right rod and reel, the correct strength line, the best-tied knots, the sharpest hooks. It is as easy as it is important, because you can be sure of those things no matter how experienced you are. For tarpon I can't stress adequate tackle enough. You see so many tarpon fishermen frogging around with light tackle, showing off, trying to set records. I used to be guilty myself, though for a third reason. I believed I gave the fish a better chance—and myself an extra thrill—with light equipment. But all reasons for using understrength tackle are dumb, and I'll tell you why. First, you break fish off, or you hurt them and then break them off, and that can ruin your day and maybe the fish's life. With the right tackle, the proper test line—no more, no less—you don't lose as many fish and you can make the fight shorter on those you do catch, and in both instances the fish gets a better shake.

If that's not reason enough, put it on selfish terms. The first fifteen minutes of a tarpon fight—a fight with *any* big-game fish—is the real joy. The first fifteen minutes and the last fifteen minutes. Those are the fun times. The in-between is usually a pain in the neck and other parts of the body. A lot of crane work and a lot of drudgery.

People who brag about three- and four-hour fights have seen too many reruns of *The Old Man and the Sea.* It may be noble, but it ain't sport. I have never taken longer than forty minutes to bring in a tarpon, either on a fly or on spinning. The biggest I ever caught on a fly weighed 132 pounds, and it took twenty-eight minutes. (As another example, the biggest Atlantic salmon I ever caught was twenty-six pounds, and it took less than fifteen minutes.)

What do you accomplish by playing tug-of-war with a tarpon for a couple of hours or more? Well, to begin with you'll probably wear yourself out, but you'll survive. If there's a big black-tip shark in the area picking up the vibrations of a floundering fish, the tarpon might not. He could easily wind up an hors d'oeuvre. All you have done then is kill a great fish neither you nor any other angler will ever get pleasure from again. The tarpon won't like it much, either.

To be sure, records are set by anglers using tackle lighter than it ought to be. But records aren't the fun or skill of fishing. A third of them may be legitimate enough, but a third are sheer luck—the right fish at precisely the right time. And a third are lies. Sometimes white

Adequate gear is imperative when fishing for tarpon because your tackle is sure to take a beating.

The tarpon's mouth is like the inside of a cast-iron stove; you must set your hook firmly.

lies, mainly about line strength, but lies nevertheless. The records-logging process is just not the most scientific thing in fishing.

I don't see records as an angler's goal at all. The odds alone make it prohibitive. Of all the fish I've caught, only two could have been records had I been using lighter tackle, because they were easy fish. One was the 132-pound tarpon I hooked with 15-pound test; 12-pound would have done the job, and it would have been a record. Another was a 1,235-pound marlin I caught in Peru. I could easily have taken it on 80-pound test, making it the largest caught in the world at the time. But we were using 130-pound. I was satisfied. It was a memorable day. I don't recall losing any of the bigger fish I have had on—sailfish, blue marlin, black marlin, tuna, tarpon, and so on. There just weren't any records among them. For me that's satisfying enough and a lot more satisfying than guessing about the big one that broke off or cursing the tackle for the limits I knew it had in the first place.

I had some guys fishing for tarpon with me at Homosassa Springs one time who deliberately used inadequate tackle, for reasons I did not ask. I let it go for a day, watching them break fish off, hurt fish. The next day I rigged 'em up with the proper lines and leaders—tougher, better—and they got seven out of the eight fish they struck. One of them said, "Gee, that's the best fishing I ever had," and the other one said, "This is the most fun I ever had fishing." They both were guides.

That's what adequate tackle is all about.

The last ten years or so have seen great advances in equipment, and the result has been that now fully 80 percent of those anglers who actively fish tarpon by sight use fly rods. The new, lighter graphite rods give you all the strength you need, and they're terrific. And they're tarpon rods, not bass rods you have to make do. I used to be 100 percent spinning, but now every ten times I go out for tarpon, nine will be with a fly rod. There's no comparison in the pleasure you get casting for them and playing them and seeing them take a fly.

The Gold Cup tarpon tournament, which I helped start in Islamorada in the 1960's, was originally open to all three kinds of casting tackle—fly, spinning, and plug. The only requirement was fifteen-pound line (fifteen-pound tippet in fly). But one year a guy who, as Vic Dunaway put it, "couldn't throw a fly past his ear" won the Gold Cup by blind casting in the deep channels with a plug rod, and we eliminated the plug and spinning from the allowances. It's now the Gold Cup Tarpon Fly Championship. Dunaway calls it "the premier flycasting competition in the world." He may not be far off.

The records of tarpon caught on a fly have gone up steadily since Joe Brooks's 148-pounder in 1961. Brooks' guide, Stu Apte, caught a 154-pounder on twelve-pound tippet in 1971, and then a 155-pounder on fifteen-pound in 1975, then a world record. Billy Pate of Islamorada set the record for tarpon caught on a fly at Homosassa in 1980 with a 182-pounder, and since then a 186-pounder has been recorded.

Everybody has his own stories when it comes to equipment, and there's no doubt that a glass rod will save you a few bucks over the lighter, better graphite, but the graphite makes it a little easier to cast. I use a nine-foot graphite rod, with twelve- or thirteen-weight floating line. That's adequate. As a measure you should be able to lift fifteen pounds of dead weight off the floor from the butt end of your tarpon rod. You need twelve or thirteen weight line to create the inertia necessary to cast a fly with a 4-0 or 5-0 hook. Either that or get a helmet, because it'll hit you in the head.

But you don't have to spend a fortune on rods. For the beginner a good glass saltwater fly rod can be bought for less than $50, and a comparable Shakespeare reel for around $75. Extra money spent on a good reel is good insurance. The better you get, the more you'll want to spend, as much as $500 for a custom-made graphite rod and a hand-machined reel or a little less for the components to build your own. Shop around, but be sure to specify that you're looking for tarpon gear. It makes a difference.

A good-sized tarpon can take all the line you have and more, so I put at least 200 yards of backing on the reel, braided Dacron testing out to twenty-five to thirty pounds. I tie that to ninety feet of No. 12 fly line with a whip finish. Then I tie on a six-foot butt leader of sixty-pound monofilament with a nail knot. I make a perfection loop the diameter of a pencil on the other end and tie it to the strength measure, a two-foot tippet of fifteen-pound mono, a Bimini twist loop tied on both ends. I tie to the perfection loop with a clinch knot, going through the bottom and back through the top with a double barrel knot. Then I tie the bottom end of the leader through a loose knot on my 100-pound shock tippet and tighten that down against the Bimini twist. Then I tie the tippet with three half hitches and a whip finish of four wraps. I tie the lure on with a perfection loop.

Obviously you can't tie such a rig in a couple of minutes. The angler with foresight ties several spares in advance, from the tippet forward. That way you're ready if you break a line or catch a fish that frays the leader or if you just want to change lures. For a tackle-busting fish you ought to be prepared for anything.

The rig that tests fifteen pounds is the minimum for tarpon—it's light enough for the best sport but strong enough for a heavy drag when you need to muscle a big fish with super strength. Guys who fish for tarpon with ten-pound test on spinning or ten-pound test leader on a fly don't get any sympathy from me when they have to twiddle their thumbs while the fish decides what happens next.

On spinning I use a seven-foot stiff tarpon rod with 15-pound test monofilament line. For leader I tie three feet of doubled 15-pound line with a Bimini twist, then an eighteen- to twenty-four-inch leader of 100-pound mono tied double line to the loop with a standard improved clinch knot. Again, I tie on the lure with a perfection loop.

That's a simple terminal rig. I used to use the shock line arrangement, with a rod length of forty-pound test tied to the heavy leader, but I quit doing it because it's not necessary. You don't need long leader for tarpon except when you're trolling or live-bait fishing, and even then a rod length of leader is enough. Tarpon seldom cut a line with their bodies. The only reason you need heavy leader is to keep them from fraying the line with the rough edges of their mouths. I double the line only because I want 100-percent knot strength.

Improvements in fly rods and fly line have had a marked impact on my own tarpon fishing. I estimate now that on spinning tackle I'll stick and get some action from five out of ten; if I land two of those I'm lucky. I lose two or three when the hook pulls out. By comparison, with fly I stick six out of ten and land three or four.

For both spinning and fly, I prefer a 4-0 or 5-0 hook—*sharp*, because a tarpon's bony, gristly mouth is as unyielding as the inside of a Franklin stove.

When equipment wasn't as sophisticated, we used to use bass plugs with those old wire hooks, and since the tarpon could bend them like a pretzel, we'd remove the wire hooks and put on triple-strength gang hooks. Fortunately we don't do that anymore, and also fortunately plugs are pretty much out of the picture now. I don't recommend gang hooks—doubles, trebles—under any circumstances. In the first place, they can be dangerous to cast. Second, it's actually harder to hook a tarpon with a double or treble; a good, sharp single hook is better. Worst of all, if a tarpon gets a treble hook or a double treble hook caught in his throat, he's going to suffer. It could kill him. If you must use a gang hook, at least take the barbs off or pinch them down, but I don't recommend them at all.

A single hook will do fine if you get your hooks sharp enough. Treat yourself to a good file—a round fine-toothed file is the secret, one about pencil-thick—and hone the hook from underneath the barb as well as around the outside surfaces.

The best lures now are the three- to five-inch streamers and the weighted streamer flies of a half ounce to three-quarter ounces. You don't see as many bucktails as you used to. The new streamers are really simple lures with scissor action feathers that open and close as you bump them along on the retrieve. Color is more a personal whim than anything else, but I've always preferred the hotter numbers, the oranges and yellows and reds. I've added some black in recent years. A favorite of many tarpon anglers is called Black Death, featuring black feathers and red hackle.

For spinning rigs the heads of the better lures are made of one-inch-square plastic a quarter-inch thick, instead of wood. The streamer is attached to that. There's an orange and black one called a Skimmer that's quite effective. You don't need any more weight than the one-quarter to a half ounce to three-quarter ounces of the weighted fly to cast a spinning rig, and it'll be plenty to get it down when you need to go down. Use as light a lure as you can cast with fifteen- or twenty-pound line.

The streamer flies have been around, of course. Their popularity has just been a tad late arriving. One of the first and biggest tarpon thrills I got was coming down one year when I was still playing baseball and catching three on a streamer for a film. It was before spring training, and I really didn't have that much time. But I used a fly rod with a big yellow and red streamer fly and caught an eighty-seven-and-a-half-pounder in about thirty minutes—at the time I think the biggest ever taken on a fly—then a seventy-five-pounder in twenty minutes, then another of about seventy pounds.

The Conditions

Tarpon are in Florida waters year round, but the ideal fishing begins in mid-March. Jimmie Albright has found that the biggest fish around Islamorada are caught from mid-April to mid-May and the most fish from mid-May to mid-June. The former will run as big as 200 pounds; the latter, around 150. The average is 70 to 80 pounds. They drop in size after the spawning season, which apparently begins in mid-May. For me in Islamorada the best month is June. The water's down and there's not as much boat traffic. At Homosassa Springs I'd fish May and June.

Active tarpon fishing continues through July and then fades until

November when those that migrate start working back into deeper water. No matter the time or place you don't see the vast schools you used to see. When Albright first started guiding in the 1940s tarpon runs frequently numbered a thousand fish or more. Now when a big school, and *none* are that big anymore, comes in off the Atlantic, twenty or thirty boats rake through 'em, and you're lucky to find a run of even a hundred fish. Most of the time they're moving in fours and fives.

Florida guides believe there are two strains of tarpon, a migratory tarpon and a dock tarpon, the latter usually found hanging around bridges in up to twenty feet of water year-round. The guides are less eager to fish for them. They call it dredging, and there's really not much sport in it. You also see tarpon consistently off Flamingo and along the Tamiami Trail on the edge of the Everglades between Miami and Tampa in both brackish and fresh water. In the winter when the water temperature drops below seventy, they search out deeper areas but don't migrate.

I don't like to fish tarpon three or four days before the full moon or three or four after. The fish are nocturnal and they aren't as active and don't take as well during the day during those times. I prefer the build to the moon, to the first half or three quarters. Tarpon move when the tide is moving in and tend to be more stationary at full high and full low.

I like a southeast to southwest wind but not more than ten or fifteen knots. The southeast is prevailing on the Florida Keys, and fish act better in prevailing wind. When the wind changes, it shakes them up. When the wind is out of the northwest to northeast, tarpon tend not to hold. They move into deeper water. I also prefer a steady barometer; a low barometer is not good.

Ideal water depth for angling from a staked-off open boat would be four to eight feet, preferably along the inlets where you can see the sandy bottom or along a slight drop-off or bank. In Florida Bay you might fish depths of up to twelve feet, but I'd draw the line there. A spot where you and the guide can see them cruising under the surface as well as when they roll is ideal. Unlike bonefish, the ultimate flat forager, you don't catch tarpon just in feeding circumstances. You get them betwixt and between—they may be eating, they may just be cruising. They roll because in their prehistoric development they grew a bladder that acts as a lung. They come up to take air into the lung when there isn't enough oxygen in the water, evidently. This makes it possible for them to travel through warmer water with the lowest oxygen content.

The Angling

As I said, the preference for anglers nowadays is to fish tarpon with a fly rod. The big factor is the new graphite rods, but another improvement is in shooting line because it now allows you to speed up your casts, to get the lure out quicker, retrieve it and cast quickly again. I don't use sinking line for that reason. With moving tarpon you want to be able to retrieve and cast again before they're out of reach. Floating line gives you that advantage. A lot of guys use sinking line, but on the retrieve they have to strip six or eight times, then maybe roll cast to get it going, and by the time it's back out there it may be too late. The fish don't wait.

As it is, even floating line, together with the weight of the lure, will get you down where the tarpon are, to where they cruise. It'll sink as much as a foot or two feet anyway. Sometimes if you're not alert enough on your retrieve it'll be raking along the grass before you know it. If you find you just can't hack the floating line, you might try floating line with a sinking tip as the first alternative. The important thing is that you get the lure where the fish are.

Ideally I'd say in five to eight feet of water you'd want the lure to run six inches to a foot beneath the surface. If you see fish running deeper, you can let it settle; if they're more on top, with floating line you're already there so there's no adjustment needed.

People who think you're a hero if you catch a tarpon on a fly rod only think that because they haven't learned to cast a fly themselves or haven't see the kinds of rods available. They're much heavier than bass bug rods and are capable of landing a 300-pound fish. As a matter of fact it's actually easier to catch a tarpon on a fly rod than any other artificial tackle. Two precautionary measures to think about: one, always make sure the reel handle is away from you when you cast so that the line won't catch on the handle. Fly line has a tendency to do that when you're shooting it out. Two, when you retrieve, always reach out over the gunwale of the boat to get the lure. Don't let the fly bang against the boat and maybe dull the hook.

If possible set up where you're not looking into the sun or the glare off the water. Wear good Polaroid sunglasses attached to a tether around your neck. They're invaluable. You're not always going to see that clearly, but give yourself every chance. If the guide has picked your spot, watch and learn what he watches for. The shadows that move like a fleet of small gray submarines in the water, the dorsal fins making furrows on top. When you see a roll, it could be the fish has been disturbed, or it could have come up for air. When it's the latter you can usually see little bubbles coming up in its wake.

The tarpon takes differently than either the salmon or the bonefish. The salmon comes up to the fly with a positive but leisurely roll; the bonefish, feeding on the bottom, usually takes it there with less fanfare. The tarpon hits with an explosion, making a jumplike move on the fly and then turning with a big boil. It is not nearly as spooky as the bonefish or as finicky as the salmon. Many times you can put a fly right on a tarpon's nose or a foot or so in front. Plugs, when they were the more popular lure, tended to spook tarpon when you got too close.

The speed the tarpon is moving and his depth in the water are, of course, contingencies. When he's moving fast or running deep, you have to be farther in front, five to ten feet, maybe more. You will get the feel of it the more you cast.

An absolutely perfect cast is one where you straighten out the length of the fly line you've stripped to the precise spot you want the fly. With tarpon you can sometimes get a little help from the tide, but you still try for that. A typical cast for tarpon is in the sixty- to seventy-five-foot range. You'll be using fairly heavy lures, so don't expect more than that very often. When the wind is up, you might have to sacrifice distance anyway, but sixty feet will usually suffice.

Under the best conditions I sometimes double haul and stretch it to eighty or even ninety feet if I see fish. On the 132-pounder, I made an eighty-foot cast with an old bass rod, and it was right in front of the tarpon's nose. He was by himself and cruising fast. Two little twitches of the fly and he had it. Jimmie Albright still talks about that cast.

There is, of course, no scent to entice them with an artificial lure, so you have to do it with action. The absolute first requirement is to get his attention. Stir him up, make him want to take it. If you have the fly in the right spot, give it a couple of bumps, move it to get him interested. This is true of all fish, but when you're moving the fly for tarpon you do it with eight- to fifteen-inch strips.

The trick, when you've got his attention, when he's *really* excited and you see him surging, is to give it three little staccato bumps—zip, zip, zip. Then at the last moment relax the line so that it won't be tight when he takes the lure. That's the pattern, and it holds true with all fishing. If he follows with a flourish, he'll take it. If he refuses, you might change the pattern a little. Cast again. Maybe strip slower. Strip faster. Don't be afraid to try anything, but always use those three or four little bumps when he's coming at it.

You would prefer a tarpon, or a bonefish, or any fish, not to take a completely tight line, if you can help it. With spinning gear it's almost impossible for that not to happen. But you can give yourself some leeway by dropping the tip and throwing a little slack in the line. With a fly rod the slack is practically built-in.

All fish make a rolling turn when they take a bait. If they take it on too tight a line, they don't get a chance to grab it as well. An Atlantic salmon creates his own slack by coming up to a fly, and you have slack built-in because the fly is swinging with a curve, but that's an exception. If you're too quick with a fish on a taut line, or if you just tick him when you get the pull, you're likely to lose him. This happens a lot with tarpon on spinning tackle because the hardness of the tarpon's mouth makes it difficult to set the hook.

When a tarpon hits a fly, you can expect him to strike hard. You will have to contend with that stripped line, that slack, to get it on the reel, but as he moves to do this, he gives you the chance to really set the hook. You do it this way: when he takes the fly, you come straight up with your rod hand; simultaneously with the other hand, even if holding some of the line you've stripped, you yank down hard and fast, pulling the line through the guides. This crucial double action should sink the tip of the hook into his jaw at least enough to hold temporarily. If the tarpon jumps immediately, he still might slip it, but if he rolls, you've got that slack from the stripped line to work with.

Be careful as he takes that stripped line. It comes up through the guides very fast and can easily foul. As a little added precaution, instead of stripping line down by my left foot into the boat, I rig a canvas basket, homemade but effective, to my hip and let it accumulate there—less chance of tangling up and better for the line.

Now comes the part where that carefully sharpened hook pays dividends. The tarpon has engulfed the lure and taken up the slack. You feel the tension, and it's time to anchor the hook in that cast-iron jaw. Fly rod or spinning, the technique then is the same. You ram it home with three hard whips of the rod, jerking back against the fish's flight. Each hit should send the hook a little further home. The tarpon'll do the rest. He'll be off and jumping, taking screaming line with him.

To play a jumping fish—and the tarpon is king of that breed—you always hold your rod high. That's so you can keep pressure on and still have line available to make a move when he makes a move. That's so you can keep the pressure on and still bow to him. The old theory, though, that you always bow to a jumping fish is baloney. With tarpon you have to be flexible.

If he jumps and you see the line come out of the water so that it's almost straight to his jaw, he could throw the hook or break it off with a twist of his head. In that case you do bow to him. Drop the point of your rod. Give him some working room.

If he jumps straight up, you might bow or you might not do anything. Keep your rod up and pay attention. How he comes down may determine his and your next move. If it appears he might flip over on the line, drop the tip, create slack. If he jumps going away from you, all you do is point the rod right at him. There is a remote chance he will come down on the line in either case, so you have to watch it's not too taut then. If he's jumping and heading toward you, the best thing to do is reel like hell.

I seldom fish for tarpon from an anchored boat, unless I'm over a bottom that is rock hard. Find your spot, set your pole in the water, and stake out. A 100-yard run is nothing for a big tarpon. He'll run right off the spool if you're anchored down or not alert. Your guide or your fishing companion should be ready to track him with the boat, either by releasing the line and poling, or by untying from the pole and letting the boat move. Tarpon usually run with the tide, unless they're scared, and then there is no telling, so the second is a good alternative. If you're alone, that might be the only way.

There is no delicate way to play a tarpon. Be ready to slug it out— to keep the pressure on, to keep him struggling for breathing room, to turn him and turn him again as soon as you can. Your drag should be set at three to four pounds initially, and you should be alert to change it on the reel when a fish is on. As the line goes off the reel, diminishing the diameter of the circle, the drag naturally increases. When you're down to half a spool, for example, the drag could easily double to six or eight pounds. When the fish is weakened, you can increase drag by pressing your thumb on the spool as you pump the rod, if you think the opportunity is right—if for instance he is no longer quite as strong as he was at the beginning, when you feel the starch going out of him.

Applying constant pressure on a tarpon will get the job done with minimum time and maximum efficiency—quicker and neater. It should exhaust neither you nor the fish, not completely anyway. When he's not pressured, the tarpon has great recuperative powers. The hairy part comes when you've got him close to the boat preparatory to landing or cutting loose. At that point he will obviously have lost considerable vinegar, and you can drag by palming the spool or thumbing the line. But keep in mind how powerful he is, how often he surprises anglers with still another burst of energy. Keep the full bend of the rod in the opposite direction of his line of movement. That's the key to finishing him. When he turns under that pressure, immediately switch over and apply it in the other direction, turning him again.

The mistake the average angler makes is reeling the same way the fish is going once he thinks the battle's over. This gives the fish a chance to get oxygen, maybe swing out for another run, or dive under the boat. If he dives, don't panic. You can work the tip of the rod around the boat.

When he's ready for the gaff, the duty belongs exclusively to the guide. If you're alone, though, or with a buddy, the gaffing technique is important to know. For the easiest release use a short-shank lip gaff and bring the point up through the gristlelike area of the tarpon's lower lip. If you think you might want to keep him, use a longer gaff and aim for the shoulders or the back of his head behind the gills.

Only when you're absolutely positive you want him for a trophy do you bring a tarpon into the boat. Otherwise you're risking big trouble. Even in a weakened state tarpon have been known to wreak havoc with anything that's not tied down, including the angler. There are tales of guys being killed by thrashing tarpon, and I believe them. If all you're trying to do is salvage your lure, forget it. Take it out while you've got him gaffed and hanging over the side, or if that becomes difficult, leave it as a remembrance. Simply cut the leader as close to the mouth as possible. The more you fool around, yanking and tearing, the less chance he has of surviving.

Another reason for not putting a tarpon in the boat is that you might be tempted to keep it there. What's the sense? You're not going to eat it. Unless it's a real prizewinner, you're not likely to mount it either. Killing it is a total waste. Fortunately I've found that the feeling for conservation runs high with tarpon fishermen. And the guides I know do a good job reminding those who don't have that appreciation. The percentage of releases gets higher every year.

So just tip your hat to him and send him on his way. You'll be surprised at the pleasure you'll get doing it. Releasing a great fish is just about the biggest thrill I get from fishing. Once you let that first big fish go, you'll find it easier and easier, and it'll carry over to your other fishing. I've kept less than a dozen tarpon of the many I've caught, and most of those were in tournaments. Considering the thrills tarpon have given me, it is only fitting.

Williams and Albright were already a tarpon-fishing team thirty years ago. Here Ted has made his cast and is anticipating a strike as he strips line.

The bend of the rod indicates whether the proper angle of playing the fish has been achieved.

Angle of rod is especially important when the fish is close to the boat.

A leaping tarpon is a thrilling sight, often occurring so close to the boat that you can feel the spray.

Note that the rod is almost straight when the tarpon is in the air. When a tarpon jumps, Ted bows the rod to it slightly to take the pressure off. When the fish is close and there is little room for stretch of the line, a hot tarpon will easily break a too-tight line.

Ted lands a big tarpon by himself, using a short-shank gaff into the fish's lower lip. This method allows the angler to retrieve his lure before releasing the fish, but Ted would prefer to cut the leader and let fish and lure go. It is safer all around.

Ted pulls in a 120-pounder.

This big tarpon was caught with a fly rod, now Ted's tackle preference for tarpon "nine out of ten times."

2

FISHING FOR BONEFISH

The Experience
with Ted Williams

Bonefish had been Ted Williams' excuse to take up residence on the Florida Keys, but in the years I had known him they had enlivened only our conversation. We had turned them over frequently there, to no hard conclusions, at least on my part. I felt that was unsatisfactory research. In the words of a Bahamian smack fisherman of long acquaintance, "Debate is not de same as in de boat." There was no comparing notes with Williams, because my notes were limited, if you can call nonexistent limited. I did, however, have prejudices. If that small a fish (a ten-pounder is a prize bonefish, and the record is only nineteen pounds) also is inedible and makes a less than awesome, not to say colorless, mount, why bother?

But I was open to persuasion, knowing it was a prejudice born of ignorance. I had fished bonefish only once, as part of an exercise to see how much hunting and fishing a small group of peripatetic sportsmen could cram into a week around Andros Island and the Tongue of the Ocean in the Bahamas. To say that I had gotten a taste would be to characterize a crack in a sidewalk as a geological fault. The first impression was all but lost in a mix of hectic activity.

On Andros we had hunted wild boar and teal, and around the Berry Islands and Joulter Cays we had gone for tarpon, and then we had fished the blue waters of the New Providence Channel for marlin. We got tarpon and marlin and duck but no boar, and at night from the bridge of our chartered boat we watched the glow of the fires from the interior of Andros where the natives still practiced Obeah magic. Then Bill Curtis, the leader of the party and a respected guide, had taken us to try for bonefish.

Williams had told me what a terrific reputation Bill Curtis had around South Florida. A one-eyed part-Indian from Hangnail, Oklahoma, Curtis had come to Miami in the early 1950's, a professional photographer. One day he had gone bonefishing. He never stopped going bonefishing. In 1960 or thereabouts he found a safe, dry place for his cameras and took out a guide's license.

At Morgan's Bluff on Andros Curtis rang in a black native named Rudy Knowles to take us to the bonefish, ostensibly teeming on the mud (west) side of the island. We fished there only one day. My recollections run together. There was some early confusion as to who was guiding whom. Bait, I recall, was a touchy subject. An engaging fellow who admitted to seven children and three "woman" but no wives, Knowles expressed a strong preference for crushed crab over the handsome lures Curtis broke out for the occasion. They argued as to who would do what with which while we waited on a great hot slab of shallow water for the advance of the bonefish.

I told Ted of these things later when we were preparing to go to Costa Rica for tarpon fishing with Vic Dunaway, the Miami-based angler-writer, and George Hommel, the Islamorada guide. I recounted the sparse impressions bonefishing had left me.

The broad, noiseless skillet of gin-colored water where the main event took place.

On the horizon the shimmering olive-drab mangroves, low slung and dead looking.

Eyes stinging with sweat, squinting onto the skillet for signs and signals.

The surface eventually scarring with dorsal fins and fluttering tails as the feeding bonefish advanced, at times from all sides.

Spasmlike strikes, more tentative than terrifying.

The high whine of a fast-diminishing reel as line peeled off at shocking speed. (The strikes gave no hint of such ferocity.)

That was about it. I had caught seven of the nine I had hooked, none of any size, five pounds tops, and later I could not even remember if I had used Rudy's crushed crab or Curtis's trendy bucktails. I suspect the former. It was Rudy's ball park.

If that is all I had gotten from the exercise, Ted said, I had better go back for a refresher as soon as possible. He threatened to take me, "as soon as you learn to tie a Bimini twist, the only difficult knot you have to know."

We spent a week in Costa Rica, fishing for tarpon at the mouth and along the tributaries of the Parismina River. I caught the first one, a seventy-pounder, and Ted caught none that day, so I bet him I'd have the most by week's-end if he spotted me four more. I may not know

The happy result of a quick, fierce bonefish battle.

how to fish, but I know how to bet. He agreed and gradually made up ground until on the last day he had caught his ninth tarpon, and I won the bet by getting my fifth. A dubious but profitable ten-dollar victory.

The Costa Rican guides told Dunaway they had never seen an angler—Ted, of course—hand out such exquisite punishment on a spinning rod. He brought in one fifty-pound tarpon in five minutes. Dunaway himself said he had never seen "such intensity or all-out dedication." It was the first time he had fished with Ted. One night when we were playing poker at the crude lodge overlooking the river, Vic asked Williams, who was not playing poker but fussing with his tackle, if it was tarpon that got him fishing in Florida. Ted said no, it was snook. I looked up from a somewhat passive poker hand, surprised.

"I'd read an article by Ray P. Holland that said a ten-pound snook tied tail-to-tail to a twenty-pound muskie would pull the muskie all over the lake," Ted said. "Well, I'd fished for muskie and I thought it was a helluva fish, so snook must be a great fish. I came down with a buddy of mine in the Marine air corps, Bob Varner. He's a federal judge now, in Jackson, Mississippi. We were stationed at Pensacola at the time, as instructors—this had to be 1943—and we saved up our gas ration stamps to buy enough gas to get us to Everglades City.

"Boy, talk about eager, we fished all day long up and down the Tamiami Trail. I wore leggings and a .22 Woodsman in a shoulder holster for snakes, and the very first or second cast I got a fifteen-pound snook. It took off like nothing I'd ever had on freshwater equipment. At first I thought it was an alligator. I'd been fishing bass and walleyed pike, and that snook would'a' ripped the tail off either of 'em.

"So we had a good day, twenty or thirty snook, and we were at this fish house at Everglades City, and I said to the guy behind the counter, 'Gee, we caught a lot of fish today,' and the guy said, 'Bring 'em in, we'll buy 'em.' 'How much do you pay?' 'Eleven cents a pound.' The next day we kept every snook we caught, and we had 110 pounds of snook, which is quite a little haul of snook. And that's the first and only and last time I ever sold fish."

My poker hands had been consistently inoperative, and Hommel and the other cutthroats were taking full advantage, so I returned my attention to the game. Show me an easily distracted poker player and I'll show you an empty pocket. But later I asked Ted if he hadn't told me it was bonefish, not snook, that first drew him to Florida.

"To the Keys," he said. "Bonefish drew me to the Florida Keys. But that was afterward. The snook started it, and the tarpon in the canals. After the service I made up my mind I was going to come down a week early just to fish before spring training. I found out a week wasn't even close to being enough. The next year I came a month early, then two months, and before I knew it I was living in Miami.

"One night I was coming home, hadn't had too good a day, hadn't been using a fly rod much then, and wasn't doing so well with plugs, and I saw this guy on the Tamiami Trail. Gee, he had a nice fish on a fly rod. I'd been casting my arm off with those plugs. I stopped the car and went back, and here's this ten-pound snook. I got him to show me the fly, and it was very simple—two feathers turned against one another to form a little 'u' and a hackle. That was it.

"We started talking. Turned out he was an old Army colonel. He said he'd been catching a lot of little tarpon up in those bilateral canals. Said he was getting so many his arms were tired. I thought he was bulldozing me, but I told him I'd give him a new reel—I saw he was using an old beat-up one, and it just so happened I had two new reels with me—if he'd tell me where his spot was, and he agreed, and I went back the next day, and sure enough they were there. From then on I used nothing but a fly rod in the Tamiami area because it's two to one, it's *ten* to one, more effective than spinning gear around all those little bushes."

I asked him if he bought the flies or was tying his own.

"My own. I loved to fly cast even then—I had Heddon rods, South Bend rods, *bamboo* rods, and a B-level or a C-level line. And I loved to make my own flies. I'd been doing it since the World Series in 1946. It added so much more enjoyment to my fishing, and I caught a heck of a lot more fish, too. I got some snook on flies and then the tarpon, and as far as I'm concerned, it was the ultimate fishing. And that was right about the time they first started catching bonefish on a fly."

"Who did? You did?"

"No. Don't rush the story. A fellow named Lee Cuddy, an outstanding fisherman, told me I oughta try bonefish on the Keys. He talked about the blue water, the clean, clear water, the pretty areas. The Keys weren't so spoiled then. Joe Brooks had gone down in 1947, and asked Jimmie Albright if bonefish would take a fly. Brooks had been mainly a bass fisherman. Jimmie said yes, and the first day Brooks caught three on a fly. And, of course, Brooks is a writer, so the word got around.

"That winter I came to Islamorada, and I caught sixty-seven bonefish. And Lee Cuddy says, 'Why not move to the Keys.' And Red Greb was egging me on. Red was a Miami angler with a reputation for tying flies. He had a wooden leg. He didn't get around too good, but he was a great fisherman. And before long I had myself a house and I was permanent."

"So? The bonefish were everything Cuddy said they were?"

"And more."

"Maybe it's time you took me bonefishing," I said.

He looked up from the tarpon leader he was rigging. "When you learn how to cast," he said, turning up the side of his mouth.

"I thought you said a Bimini twist."

"Bonefishing requires precision casting."

"I want to do it in this lifetime," I said.

"Practice," he said.

After that we had hunted in Zambia. Ted had won the American League Manager of the Year award for almost taking the Washington Senators out of their misery—no one could do that, as it turned out—and he was rewarding himself for putting up with the job.

We both shot sable antelope near the Kafue River, and then we split tacks for three days. Ted went up the Zambezi and shot kudu and

JOHN MAHONY

In the late 1940's, getting a bonefish on a fly was considered a feat. Fishing with Lee Cuddy, Ted got this one off Elliott Key, near Miami.

Cape buffalo, and while he was there fished for tiger fish. I heard the hunters talking about tiger fish and bragging about its fighting prowess. When he got back, that night in the tent, I asked Ted for a critique. He said, "It's a good enough fish. A good fish, but for its size it's not great. Nothing like a bonefish."

"There you go again with bonefish," I said.

"Yeah, and I'm going to take you bonefishing, too," he said. "As soon as you learn how to tie a few flies."

68

Eventually, inevitably, our schedules settled down at just the right time, and late one April I found myself "along for the ride" when the bonefishing season had him in a tow. By then he had given up managing major-league baseball teams "for all time," and was taking advantage of his leisure by fishing as if it were his livelihood. In the meanwhile I had read up on bonefish, trying to build some enthusiasm. I found it inspired more than casual praise from more than casual fishermen.

J. B. McFerran had caught the first bonefish with rod and reel in 1891 near Miami and had written, "I verily believe that pound-for-pound the bonefish is, far and away, the king of all swimmers, and the only objection I can urge against him is that an experience with him forever disqualifies one for all other fishing." Stanley Babson had written an entire book on bonefish. Irving S. Cobb said that "next to a Vermont Democrat the bonefish is the gamest fish I ever met." Zane Grey compared it to "dynamite and chain lightning."

Grey said he had been told beforehand that he should "not go after bonefish unless you can give up all other fishing." He had gone anyway, risking it, and said he found the fish to be "the wisest, shyest, wariest, strangest fish I ever studied." He said he believed "no salmon, no barracuda, no other fish celebrated for swiftness of motions" was in the same class.

Then Grey said a surprising thing. He said bonefish was "the best food fish I ever ate." I could not imagine that. I had tried bonefish once or twice and, aside from the filings of anatomy it threw into every dangerous bite, found it to be a drab experience. I had read that the Japanese grind them into fishcakes, and I knew that some early Conchs ate bonefish, but I passed these off as acts of desperation. Some societies eat almost anything when times are tough.

Joe Brooks, the modern piscine archivist, wrote about bygone Keys natives foraging onto the flats for their dinner, catching the bonefish while *they* dined. Bonefish feed almost exclusively on the flats and shallows, their cigar-shaped silver bodies nose down into the mud, their translucent tails flapping on the surface, their suckerlike mouths, the upper jaw overlapping the underslung mouth, rooting around for sand worms and crunching up fiddler crabs and mollusks and other crustaceans. Brooks told of a Conch named Pinder who could take a three-tined spear called a grains and hit a tailing bonefish from thirty-five feet.

Mr. Pinder's neighbors, however, were more likely to walk out on the flats at low tide and let the bonefish have it with twelve-gauge shotguns—food fishing at its most practical. Modern Conchs do not do those things, of course. They let the paying customers come down from New Jersey to fish for them with conventional tackle and help the islands prosper. If they're eating bonefish now, they're doing it on the sly. With lots of catsup.

I told Ted the stories, but he already knew them. He said I should leave well enough alone. He said it was bad enough bonefish are netted for bait in the Bahamas—"You can troll 'em all day long in a major fishing tournament because their flesh holds up so well." If anybody ever got the notion to put them on a menu, he said, it'd be a sad day for conservation.

"With very few exceptions, an occasional mount, I never keep a bonefish. And I sure as hell don't eat 'em. Joe Brooks used to say his love for the bonefish was so great he'd sooner eat a relative."

We were putting in his skiff at a small marina on the ocean side of Key Largo, down a road almost hidden from the main highway (U.S. 1) by gumbo-limbo trees. A woman with flesh-colored hair and one of those deep-tanned young-old faces was at the counter, adjusting a halter top that was designed for a smaller load. She wanted to know if Ted was Ted Williams.

Ted said no. "But a lot of people make that mistake; I think Williams is actually a much older man."

He turned to me and said loudly, "Did you hear about that alligator biting that kid's leg off?" I said yes and what a shame it was, going along with the joke. The woman's eyes widened. Ted couldn't see it; he was looking at me, but he knew. He was still grinning when we loaded into the skiff and started up, moving briskly into the wind.

The spring tides on the Keys had been fattened up by a full moon, and with the tide coming in hard, Ted was not reluctant to take liberties with the water. At top speed we hammered out the channel and turned north along the edges of small, unlikely looking shallows and narrow inlets. We rode for ten minutes, then passed into a broader basin of shallow water, crossing over turtle grass and sea fans and croppings of coral and perilously close to a series of lobster traps. A giant manta ray, the size of the top of a car, spooked and angled away from our path.

"The best tide is half up to half out—high water," he shouted over the whine of the outboard. "Bonefish on the flats are nervous wrecks. Skittish as hell. But they aren't as skittish in high water."

"What do you consider high?"

Staked out on a bonefish flat, lure dangling, Ted and a neighbor await the first strike of the day.

"Fifteen inches to two feet, minimum," Ted said.

He abruptly turned the skiff, raising an arc of spray, and slowed the engine. We purred along the edge of a tidal creek past mangroves covered with the stark white residue of bird droppings. The windward side of the mangroves jutted out like the bottom tip of a coconut for fifty yards, then folded back and opened onto a broad, elongated flat, its breadth exposed to the sea.

"This bottom's not quite green enough for me," Ted said, looking around, "but most people would take this. I think you find bigger bonefish on greener bottoms, where there's more food. You see more of those around Islamorada. I think the bigger fish are there. But this'll be good."

He cut the engine and let the skiff glide onto the flat, crosswind but furthered along by the tide. Another stingray, smaller this time, shook itself loose from the sand it had nestled in and lumbered off the edge of the flat. The wind was up but fairly steady at ten to fifteen miles out of the southeast, a prevailing wind I knew Ted favored. The corrugated surface of the flat was not so ruffled that you could not see bottom clearly enough.

Ted picked up the push pole and carefully worked us into the interior of the parched white table. After twenty or thirty yards he set the

71

This big barracuda foraged onto a bonefish flat off the Berry Islands in the Bahamas, and paid for it. Under such conditions, barracuda make excellent sport.

pole into the mud, pushing it hard, and tied on. He straightened up on the box in the bow to survey the flat. The glare off the water, muted by a layer of high, gauzy clouds, was not nearly as intense as it would be in a couple of hours.

"Good time of year, pretty good water," he said.

"How good?"

"About fourteen inches deep, probably seventy-five degrees. They'll stay longer on the flats on a day like this. In the winter when it's cold and windy, they stay out there more"—he pointed—"in four, six feet of water. Same in the summer when it gets too hot. They come and feed and then get the hell off."

At the far corner of the flat, near a dark crease in the water's coloration, there was a small but violent combustion on the surface, then a sunburst of furrows leading from it.

"Barracuda," Ted said without excitement. "Probably chasing a small school of bonefish. They prey on bonefish. That's why I use wire leader, in case a barracuda gets interested. Barracuda can cut through monofilament like it was nothing. But they can be almost as much fun

72

as bonefish in these conditions. One time at Great Harbor Key I caught a thirty-pounder that was trailing a five-pound bonefish. It was the highlight of the trip. Don't think a barracuda is not a helluva game fish, boys."

With his legs spread and his arms akimbo, Ted rolled on the sides of his feet, settling his position. He had a spinning rod in his right hand, pressed to his hip.

"Why spinning?" I said. "I thought you preferred fly."

"Windy weather, for one thing. You get a lot of that in the spring and fall, and there's no sense beating yourself to death trying to put a fly to a spot when spinning'll do it easier. Day in, day out, spinning is the most productive way to fish for bonefish, and I have every bit as much fun playing them on spinning. I may not accomplish as much because catching anything on a fly requires more skill, but I'd guess ninety percent of the best bonefishing is done on spinning."

He was absorbed now in examining the flat. An implacable sentinel. I had seen him in this posture so many times, for such incredibly long periods, hours actually, that I instinctively relaxed. I put my hands behind my head and leaned back in the stern, the sun at my back. I

A good bonefish flat is exactly that: a habitat.

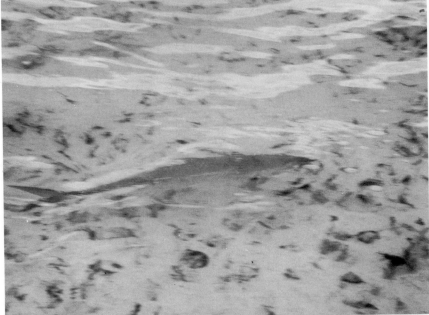

said it never ceased to amaze me how a guy famous for his impatience—flying off the handle, throwing bats and tantrums—could show more patience than anybody for a sport where success was so closely linked to long, lonely vigils.

"When I was a kid I could sit in a duck blind all day and never move," he said. "Just for that one flight of ducks. I used to sit by the road for hours waiting for that one rabbit to cross over. All morning I'd sit, then the damn rabbit would come way down the road and stop and look and run the other way."

He laughed, then got serious again.

"That's patience, sure. But I don't necessarily show great patience fishing. I'm willing to wait because I know if I do it right, things will happen. Being in the right place at the right time, being properly rigged, I know I have a helluva chance to catch a fish. But look how little patience I have with a crappy cast or a bad maneuver in a boat? Or no style, no talent for fishing, especially with a guy who's supposed to know what he's doing but doesn't.

"I know the guys I gave downs to as a flight instructor at Pensacola weren't the eager young guys just learning; they were the hotshots who were coming through, maybe instructors from someplace else, guys who were supposed to know or thought they knew but didn't. With guys like that I had no patience.

"I don't have patience with somebody in the boat who frogs around. I told you about that photographer I had taking tarpon movies that time. A good photographer, and I liked him. I put him in another boat so he could shoot. I got a tarpon on, and it was running toward my boat. Gee, it looked like it might be going to leap right in the boat. I started yelling, 'Get ready, get ready, he's going to jump in the boat!'

"Damned if he doesn't, on his first jump, right into my boat. I'm in there thrashing around trying to keep one of us from going overboard, and I yelled to the photographer, 'Did you get it? Did you get the picture?' 'No,' he said. 'I missed it.' I couldn't believe it. I told him to pack his things and get to shore. Get his rear out of there.

"I never felt I had to shoot a lot of game or catch a lot of fish to enjoy it. Being there is enough. I just like to be there. But I want to be in a nice safe boat. I want to be rigged properly. I want nice tackle. If my tackle isn't good, I don't want to fish. I want my flies to be tied properly, preferably by me. When I hunt, if the gun doesn't suit me, I don't want to shoot. Same thing."

He had the lure in the water even before I could straighten up to look. Without a word he had crouched down and lifted the rod off his hip, the little white bucktail jig with a red tip dangling, a tiny piece of fresh shrimp visibly sweetening the hook. In one motion, astonishingly quick and smooth for a man so large, he had flicked his wrist and sent the lure flying to a spot seventy feet away, toward the outer edge of the flat.

Still crouching, he waited—one beat, two beats. I looked and saw nothing on the surface except the expanding circles where the lure had dipped in. No furrows, no waggling tails, no tiny tell-tale mushroom clouds of mud, the calling cards of bonefish. Whatever he had seen was cruising underneath and not stopping for lunch.

He bumped the lure twice—twitches, he calls them—inching it forward and slightly to the left. Then he gave it three short jerks and paused, for a second or two. Suddenly he whipped the rod, setting the hook. The rod doubled. Four or five schoolmates of the fish that was now pinned to his line scattered like bits of shrapnel.

The terrified bonefish took off, and from the raveling line came a sound like wind tearing through a crack in a tin roof. Hearing that close up, from someone else's reel, for the first time made it somehow infinitely more impressive.

Ted lifted his rod high to keep the line out of the water and slightly dropped the tip and let the fish run. Forty, sixty, eighty yards before it turned. Immediately he brought the tip of the rod up and, inclining it away from the turn, began to reel.

He was standing upright now, sure in the knowledge he had this one already in the book.

"There's nothing like that first run of a bonefish," he said. "No other fish does it quite like that. There's no question a ten-pound bonefish will pull a ten-pound Atlantic salmon right down the river. For the first hundred yards he's that strong. But of course he doesn't jump, and he doesn't have great endurance. A tarpon you pretty near have to fight to exhaustion."

"That why you like this fish so much?" I asked. "That big burst out of the box?"

"That's part of it, sure. But I like it for all the other reasons, too. Picking the best spot, finding the fish, seeing them take a lure. You're not fishing blind. There's suspense to it. Skill. And you get to fish it so many ways."

"Other than this?"

"You can wade for it, but a boat is better because you can cover more ground. You can use artificial. You can use a fly. You can use bait. You can even fish out there in deep water, but there's no pleasure for me in that. A stab in the dark.

"And the tackle considerations have to do mainly with precise casting, not fish size. You probably have to cast more accurately for bone-fish than any other fish. I'm using a six-and-a-half-foot rod because it allows me to get more line out in the wind. I've got ten-pound test on because it's best for overall handling. Sometimes I use eight for smaller fish, but ten is better. Adequate tackle."

"Why not twelve then? Or fourteen?"

"Twelve-pound is not as flexible for spinning, not as easy to cast. That's going too far."

He was reeling steadily now. Less than twenty feet from the boat, the bonefish made a last desperate run. Line screamed but only for a few seconds, and Ted was on him again.

"I didn't even see 'em coming," I said. "Were they feeding or what?"

"No. There were six fish, moving pretty good. I thought for a second I might be a little late with the cast, but it was five feet in front of 'em when it hit, and the one turned on it."

"Why'd you crouch down?"

"The shadow. Anything will scare this fish. A shadow, a noise in the boat, a plane flying overhead. Scratch your arm and it'll spook. That's another reason fly casting is not as good—the false casts you have to make getting that shooting line out with the long leader. The shadows that makes. I've made casts on my knees when the sun was bad. I made a sixty-foot cast to a bonefish in ten inches of water one day, and the bait didn't scare him, but closing the bail did. Just that little click. You have to learn to close the bail quietly."

In less than five minutes he had the bonefish, a six-pounder, in the net. Compared with its first heroic run, it was docile at the finish. Ted held up the fish, hooking his fingers under the jaw, and tenderly re-moved the lure. When he put it back into the water, he held it by the tail and beneath the belly and pushed it forward, then backward, then forward again, forcing water through the gills. The bonefish came alive in his hands, turned sharply and fled.

"He'll be OK," Ted said, and, to the fish, "Thanks."

"How many's that make over the years?"

"Over two thousand bonefish," he said, "and if it was exactly two thousand, I'd hope to God one thousand nine hundred and ninety-nine were still alive."

"What would that leave, the twelve-and-a-half-pounder on your wall?"

"Yeah, I kept that one. It was a helluva fish, I wanta tell you. But I never keep a bonefish anymore."

A ten-pounder, caught on a fly.

Careful handling on the release can save a bonefish's life.

He looked around the flat again, cupping his hand over his glasses to cut the glare. Seeing nothing, he untied the line from the push pole, pulled up the pole, and began moving us toward the other side of the flat. He said he was surprised there was so little activity.

A thick, sudden band of cumulus clouds skudded over then and pulled a gray sheet across the water. The bottom dulled out and turned satiny with shadows. Ted put down the pole, and we drifted. A red speedboat with what looked to be teenagers in the cockpit blasted the silence and thundered near the flat, full speed. Ted glared. As if the driver could see him, impossible at 100 yards, the boat veered off, making a wake like a scimitar.

"I think the fish'll come, but it might still be too early," Ted said and sat down in the bow. "When all the conditions are perfect, Bush, I expect you to catch one."

Lee Cuddy watches as the bonefish revives.

JOHN MAHONY

He took a swig from a water bottle and passed it to me.

"Since you've nothing else to do," I said, "tell me about Chuck Roberts getting you started fishing as a kid."

"Chick Rotert, not Chuck Roberts. And I already told you that story."

I said I was a sucker for its Horatio Alger qualities. The eleven-year-old kid, Ted himself—his father gone a lot, his mother working the San Diego and Tijuana street corners at night for the Salvation Army—gravitating to the fishing holes and baseball fields of southern California.

"A lot of people thought Chick Rotert was a rummy or something because he used to like to drink that three-point-two beer," he said, "but as far as I was concerned he was a great man. He'd been a game warden, and he had a couple fingers shot off in World War I, and I loved him. He used to go fishing around those bass lakes near San Diego and he'd come back with pictures, six-, seven-pound bass, nice bass. I still love good bass fishing, and I was just fascinated as hell. That appealed to me, you know?

"So I finally got a rod and reel, a three-dollar and ninety-cent Pfleuger Akron reel and a Heddon bamboo rod, just a straight bamboo rod. But I will tell you one thing"—he gave me a hard look—"I went out and learned how to cast the damn thing before I went fishing with it. I learned how to use it.

"So I got my first chance to go fishing and I got some bass, not very big, and from there I tried the surf in San Diego with a wonderful man, Mr. Cassie. I played on a baseball team with his kid, and he was nuts about fishing, but his kid didn't care anything about it, so he would take me. For company, I guess.

"We'd make up two or three Calcutta rods and drive to Coronado Beach and fish the whole night for croakers or cobia. Till four in the morning we'd fish. We'd catch the tide and wade in almost to our waists and get soaking wet, but I didn't care. Surf casting was great fun. After a while I could cast as far as anybody on the beach. Then at five or so we'd head back.

"Mr. Cassie had an ulcer, and all he could eat was graham crackers, chocolates, and milk. That was his lunch. It must not have been very appetizing because after I'd finished mine he'd give me his. And then I'd conk out on him on the ride back. Here I am a young kid, and I'd go to sleep, and he'd have to make it all the way without anybody to talk to. The dearest man, a great fellow.

"From there I fished for yellowtail and tuna. I met some kids whose big brother had a boat, and I'd get a trip. I remember one time in San Diego, I'm guessing at this, in 1933 or '34, I went out on that little boat and we caught ninety-eight barracuda. Ninety-eight. We brought them back into town on ice and wrapped 'em up four to a paper, and we'd just give them to anybody on the street. Just wrap 'em up and give 'em away.

"After that I was bought by the Red Sox and shipped to Minnesota, and during that summer I had the chance to fish for walleyes up at Milac Lake. And of course I wound up on the East Coast, and got to fish New England. I caught a four hundred-pound tuna in Ipswich Bay during the season one year. I had my shirt off when the tuna hit, and I was two hours bringing it in, and that night I was burned so bad you couldn't breathe on me. The next day I had to put on that wool uniform. Geez, torture. I gobbed about a half inch of Noxzema on just so I could suit up.

"It was about that time I read the article in *Field and Stream* about snook. That's the first time I ever got interested in going to Florida, because of what Ray P. Holland said about snook."

He was up again, this time poling back down into the broad belly of the flat. I looked where he was looking. The sun had reemerged in force, and a portion of the surface was alive with fluttering tails, a school of ten or more. He waited. This time he did not set the push pole, but laid it quietly in the boat as he took up the spinning rod. I moved to watch, and he shushed me, and then he sent the lure out again, once more with breathtaking speed—a lick of flame igniting the surface forty-five feet away.

The fish were tailing. Small balloons of mud rolled up from where they dined. Ted worked the lure in front of them, but they did not take. The slight movement of the boat and the advance of the bonefish changed the angle, and he cast again. He bumped the lure—once, twice, three times, four times, making small detonations in the mud just ahead of the fish.

"The secret," he whispered, "is not to retrieve too quickly. The tendency is always to be too quick."

The fish he was after turned toward the lure. He bumped it again, this time quickly in staccato, one, two, three times. Another pause, a whip action, and again his rod doubled. This time it was a bigger fish. It had stripped more than 100 yards of line before he turned it. Just as before, however, he had it played and by the boat and into the net in less than five minutes. An eight-pounder.

When he had caught and released two more, he finally sat down in the stern of the skiff and let me fish. By now there was enough activity on the flat to almost pick and choose.

"I wanta see this," he said.

"Try not to get jealous," I said.

It was another twenty minutes before I got one on. I spooked a small school before it happened, casting directly into them. Ted made a face and looked away. Then I lofted a facsimile of a decent cast into the teeth of an advancing fish that would not be denied, and he took and ran.

As I played it, Ted advised.

Bringing in the 10-pounder with Keith. This was the first time Ted had used shrimp on spinning tackle while fishing for bonefish.

I had, of course, been "too quick retrieving, but that's OK, you've got it on, so don't worry about that now."

I was also "slow getting my rod tip down" when it ran.

I was also a little too eager bringing it up and less than smooth turning the fish.

I also did not keep the pressure on next to the boat, and that's why it ran again.

I also should have helped myself there by palming the spool, increasing the drag a little.

Finally the bonefish was in the net.

"See?" Ted said. "Nothing to it."

The Expertise:
Ted Williams on Bonefish

The Fish—and Where to Catch It

Albula vulpes . . . the White Fox . . . the Phantom of the Flats . . . the Gray Ghost. All the names and nicknames apply. But put a hook into a ten-pounder and you'll think the phantom had turned into a sidewinder missile. Pound for pound, the bonefish may be the toughest saltwater fish that swims.

There's no question in my mind that if you tied a ten-pound bonefish to the tail of a ten-pound Atlantic salmon, it would pull the salmon right out of the park. It might even tear the salmon's tail off. For the first 100 yards it is the sprint champion of fishing.

Of course, bonefish don't jump. And as game fish go, they are far from heavyweights. And you don't catch them in the prettiest surroundings. And they don't appear in the gourmet cookbooks. But for a fish that demands excellence in casting and careful attention to the most minute details of angling and at the same time can give you a battle at any weight and on almost any equipment, the bonefish is in a class by itself.

Bonefish inhabit the tidal flats and saltwater shallows of many subtropical areas, but they are a relatively new fashion in fishing circles. As a result the emphasis on their value as game fish pretty much centers on south Florida and the waters of the Caribbean.

I've caught them in Cuba and along the Yucatan peninsula of Mexico, throughout the Bahamas, the Marquesas islands, up and down both sides of the Florida Keys, and as far north as Biscayne Bay in Miami. They are also fished for in Hawaii, off Bermuda, and along the southern coast of Africa. Surprisingly, however, they are not found

84

along the Pacific Coast of the United States, in the Gulf of Mexico north of Yucatan, or along the west coast of Florida.

Like most game fish the choice locations for bonefish seem to correspond with their migration. There is no doubt they are bigger and tougher, perhaps further up the migratory ladder, in some areas of the Caribbean than others. My favorites include a number of hot spots in the Bahamas: Bimini, Cat Cay, the east end of Freeport, the Joulter Cays, Middle Bight and the "mud" side of Andros, Abaco, and Great Harbor Cay. I also like the Caicos Islands, St. Croix, and the flats off the Isle of Pines and Varedero Beach in Cuba, where I fished before Castro took power and hope to fish again some day.

But the best bonefishing I've found is right outside my door around Islamorada and the Florida Keys. The fish are generally much bigger in Keys waters than they are in the Bahamas. There is one area within a two-mile radius of Lignum Vitae Key where catches of more than a dozen fifteen-pounders have been recorded. And whereas the average bonefish is no bigger than six pounds, the average on the Florida bay side of Islamorada and near the bridge openings on the ocean side is closer to eight pounds. Some "hot spots" actually produce small potatoes. There are thousands of bonefish around Eleuthra in the Bahamas, but I never saw one that was bigger than a fat banana.

My largest bonefish was a twelve-and-a-quarter-pounder caught at Buchanan Key on the bay side southwest of Islamorada. That is a big bonefish because anything bigger than a ten-pounder is a prize. Fortunately expert documentation on where the biggest are consistently found is not available, and the hunt for record bonefish has not really accelerated. I say fortunately because both factors favor the White Fox's conservation.

In areas other than those mentioned it's clear enough that most anglers don't even know what a great fish it is. The world's record, nineteen and a half pounds, was caught by a surf caster on the west coast of South Africa. He admitted he wasn't even fishing for bonefish. It was an accident.

An attractive aspect to bonefishing is that you can do it many ways, with a fly, with artificial, with live bait, in a skiff, wading, in a larger boat, even trolling; but essentially it is a light-tackle, sight-fishing quarry for the skiff-poling angler. Some who have fished for it compare it to the permit because it moves a little like a permit, it tails, being a bottom feeder, and it is caught in practically the same locales. But I don't consider permit half as good a game fish because it is too temperamental about taking a fly. If a fish lacks the desire to take a

Another one just big enough for a quick photo, and an even quicker release.

properly presented fly, I say it doesn't measure up. You have to be in a lot of permit to get one on a fly. I haven't.

Like the tarpon much of what you read about bonefish is guesswork. Research has been sparse, and their life cycle and habits are open to conjecture. Evidently, however, they spawn almost year-round in the more tranquil warmer waters, and the eggs ride the currents and tides to predestined areas. It has been determined, for example, that bonefish eggs laid south of Cuba in the Cayman Islands hatch in the surf off Islamorada. Eggs that are spawned near Islamorada wind up hatching off St. Lucie, Florida, and are carried by the currents to the waters of Grand Bahama.

Stanley Babson's little gem of a book, *Bonefishing,* quotes Dr. Lavett Smith of the American Museum of Natural History as saying that bonefish eggs do indeed float to their hatching destinations and that the critical period of development begins just beyond the surf zones. Jimmie Albright has found bonefish eggs caught in the seaweed of an incoming tide on the ocean side of Islamorada and has picked up little bonefish, one and a half to three inches long, in specimen nets in the surf. Adult bonefish obviously develop very rapidly in those offshore waters because you never see little ones of less than a pound on the flats. One reason could be that they are difficult to see. Bonefish have shiny sides and bellies and when the light reflects off the bottom, it makes them almost transparent. Fortunately their backs give them away.

A strange thing about the bonefish life cycle: when born they look nothing like bonefish. They don't even look like fish. They look more like tadpoles. With legs. Then they go through a ribbon stage and become eellike, actually shrinking in size before assuming the cigar shape of the adult. Then the growing really accelerates. But a full-grown bonefish seldom gets more than three feet long, and when filled out their bodies are never very heavy. The Atlantic record is only about sixteen pounds.

In the water a bonefish is recognizable by the fact that it is moving all the time. Its back has a silverish-green hue, and its sides and belly are shiny white. If you don't catch it in a feeding posture, tail flapping leisurely on the surface, you can identify it out of the water by its suckerlike mouth, the snout curling over the lower jaw. Inside that mouth is a kind of built-in food processor. The tongue has a rough, pebbly surface, like mother-of-pearl glued to a stick. The roof of the mouth has three sets of crusherlike teeth used to grind up the crustaceans bonefish feed on. I've had a 3-0 hook squeezed shut in one of those crushers. I've seen lead shot distorted by them.

Bonefish can be found feeding in deeper water on skipping minnows, and it's likely they have plenty to eat out there. But their banquet table is the saltwater flat and the adjoining shallows. Only the adults come on the flats, however; you seldom see bonefish of less than a pound there. They feed during tidal changes. They usually stay deep during the falling tide, then come on with the incoming tide and feed through it. In the winter, however, they seem to prefer the warmed water left by the outgoing tide. They get off when the flat starts to rise out of the water, as some do completely, but I've seen bonefish still feeding in no more than three or four inches of water, their backs actually protruding from the surface.

The larger bonefish prefer the livelier bottoms near an inlet or a channel. They feed on little hermit crabs, shrimp, conch, halgranites, clams, seaworms and mollusks, crustaceans of every type. They even ingest a little sand to aid in digestion. The flats they frequent on the Keys tend to be the ones on the sheltered Florida Bay side, but you also find them on ones bordering the inlets coming off the ocean.

Besides that incredible first run, when they can strip 100 yards of line off a reel so fast you don't realize what's happening until it's too late, the most distinctive thing about bonefish from an angler's standpoint is that you have to treat them like high explosives. They are nervous wrecks on the flats. You can scare a bonefish by sneezing. You can spook a whole school by clearing your throat or scraping your rod on the gunwale of your boat. I've raised my voice at somebody's lousy cast and cleaned off an entire flat. Make too bold a move, cause any kind of vibration, and they're gone.

There is a disadvantage in this that isn't talked about much. The best method to fish them is standing on a tacklebox or on the small specially built platforms the guides use in a bonefish skiff, where you not only have a better view but can cast effectively to them. But up there they can also see *you* better. You risk making shadows, either from your body or your tackle. I'm convinced they can see you that well because I go through it all the time.

At six foot four when I stand on a box two feet above the waterline, I make a silhouette that is almost eight and a half feet off the water. By contrast, wading in two feet of water gives me a silhouette less than four and a half feet. That's an advantage; but it's a disadvantage, too, because it cuts your visibility way down. Wading is not the optimal way of fishing for bonefish. You see five times as many fish from a boat, standing up.

The Tackle

Joe Brooks's success with Jimmie Albright catching bonefish on a fly in 1947 first got me interested, and I still think fly fishing for a great game fish is the ultimate in tackle handling. More often than not, though, because of the conditions you encounter and the nature of the fish itself, I recommend spinning gear for bonefish.

I use ten-pound monofilament line on a fairly long, six-and-a-half- to seven-feet bonefish rod, fairly sturdy with conventional tip action. I use either fiberglass or graphite, but I prefer fiberglass because at the shorter lengths it is a little more flexible. You need flexibility because you will have to cast very quickly and very accurately; bonefish don't tarry the way a lot of fish do. They are always on the move. The longer rod, seven feet, say, gives you two advantages: you can throw more line, and when you're playing the fish and need to get line out of the water, you can lift the tip of the rod higher.

Spinning gear ready, Ted surveys the flat for telltale "muds" and fluttering tails.

Eight-pound test is all right if you're fishing in waters that rarely produce fish of more than eight pounds, something you run into often in the Bahamas. But don't kid yourself about bonefish. A five-pounder on that first mad dash can snap ten-pound line like it was nothing. When in doubt stick to ten, again out of recognizing that you must always start with adequate tackle. Twelve-pound is a little too heavy. I don't catch as many fish with twelve because I can't cast it as well.

I load up the reel with at least 185 to 225 yards of line. Again, if you don't have enough and the fish is of any size, that first run will strip you clean. Because of the frequent intrusions of barracuda and some sharks on the bonefish flats, I sometimes tip the line with a light three-inch wire, No. 2 stainless. The guides don't recommend it; they'd rather you get your lure out of the water if you think a barracuda might take it, but I have a lot of fun throwing to barracudas on a flat, especially when the bonefishing is slow.

Even if I intend to use spinning, however, I still take along a fly rod, just in case the conditions are right. I use a nine-foot, three-and-three-quarter-ounce graphite fly rod. A six-ounce fiberglass would be an alternative. The longer the rod the more line you can cast. On a fly rod I put a minimum of 150 yards of Dacron backing, testing at thirty pounds—it'll wear down to twenty, but you never have to change it—and then thirty yards of No. 9 or No. 10 line, with a shooting head and a twelve-foot tapered leader with a ten-pound tippet, three feet long. You can make a better presentation with a tapered leader. I tie it beginning with a butt leader of forty pounds, three feet long. Then two-foot lengths of thirty- to twenty- to fifteen-pound, and then the three feet of ten-pound test.

Hook size depends on depth of water, retrieving the line, and conserving the fish. I use keel hooks or hooks bent in such a way that they will ride up instead of down, because when you are bumping along the bottom in front of a bonefish you don't want to hang up on a piece of coral or a sea fan or even some grass. A must for me when bonefishing is a weedless hook. I use a No. 1 or No. 2 hook on a fly, or a 1-0 or 2-0 on spinning. If you're using bait, whole live shrimp, say, a 4-0 would be the maximum. I caught my twelve-and-a-half-pounder on a 3-0 hook using live shrimp.

I use the smaller hooks with artificial lures and the larger ones with bait because bonefish tend to gulp the hook that has bait on it. You want to guard against a fish swallowing the hook because if that happens it has less chance to survive a release. Unfortunately a hungry bonefish will take almost any size hook. I've had them bend 4-0 hooks and swallow smaller ones right down to their gullet. All you can do then at the release is cut the line off at the mouth and pray what's left doesn't strangle the fish.

One thing about bonefish in comparison, say, with tarpon is that they are both indiscriminate eaters. The bonefish has a trucker's taste and will go for just about anything you offer it, providing the presentation is proper. For almost all my bonefish lures I use a combination of colors at the tip for this reason. My preference for lures on spinning is a little white bucktail with a touch of color, red, yellow, or brown, on either the head or the butt fixed to an eighth- to a quarter-ounce lead molded with a keel. Orange and pink bucktail are also good colors. I might have been one of the first to use orange for bonefish, some thirty years ago, and I still think it gives an extra spark to pretty near any lure. A Hampson lure, with an eighth-ounce round head, white and brown bucktail, is a nice little jig. To make it even more effective, I sweeten the hook with a tiny piece of fresh shrimp.

For a fly yellow is a great color, and so is brown. Again, use a No. 1 or No. 2 keel hook that will ride up, weighted with an eighth-ounce lead so that the lure itself will glide to the bottom. I tie my flies to a light chenille body, using white bucktail with orange, brown, red, or yellow. I tie the formed end of the bucktail back toward the eye of the hook so that it will pass through grass without hanging up. That reminds me of one other general consideration for color of the lure, be it

The proper way to thread a shrimp on a 3-0 hook. For bonefish the combination is deadly.

fly or spinning: on a white sandy bottom stick to darker colors; when the bottom is darker, due to grass, for example, use light-colored lures. But white goes with everything.

I usually don't break out my fly rod until I'm fishing in about a foot of water and there's not much wind. Then you want to lay on the surface as delicately as possible, and you can do that best with fly line. The leader then becomes a big factor. I've used as much as a fourteen-foot leader. For some people that's tough to handle—to put it exactly on the line and to the distance you want—but it gives you the advantage of being able to reach a point with as little disturbance as possible. That long a leader takes getting used to. You have to use a small fly, with as little as a No. 6 hook.

I don't recommend fishing for bonefish in deep water from anchored boats or bridges. It takes nine tenths of the joy out of it and at least that much of the skill. But it is done. The usual way is with bait-casting rods and a free running reel, ten-pound test or more, doubled at the leader, and a bait of either live shrimp, crab, cut mullet, or conch. Chumming the waters beforehand with sardines is recommended for this method too, and it is a reasonable way to go for fish that you're going to eat. But you're not going to eat bonefish, so why do it?

The Conditions

A good bonefish flat is a good bonefish flat year-round, but there are times when the fish are much more cooperative. My favorites are late spring to early summer, mid-March through May and even into June, and then the early fall, October, although I usually miss the latter because I'm still up in New Brunswick then, fishing for Atlantic salmon. The ideal water temperature for bonefish on the flats is seventy-five to eighty degrees, and these times of the year pretty much guarantee those temperatures. Real cold weather can be an exception because the deeper water might be sixty-five degrees and the flat seventy, and they'll come up in that.

When it gets too hot in the dog days of summer, or when it's cold and windy in the winter, the bonefish come on and get off the flats in a hurry; they spend more time outside in deeper water where fishing for them changes so radically it is no thrill at all.

I prefer a flat where two or three feet of water is available at high tide. That's ideal for spinning tackle. For fly casting it has to be shallow, I'd say from ten inches to two feet, because you're more on top with a fly, more delicate with the presentation. In water that shallow bonefish really get spooky. I've fly-fished for them in less than six inches of water without having them scatter. When the depth goes over two feet, though, I'd recommend switching to spinning.

Unlike the tarpon, which is a mid-water swimmer, the bonefish is a bottom swimmer. You're not wasting your time when you're fishing for them in four feet or more, but you won't see them as well and they won't give you clear signals. Sometimes you get a large school, numbering 100 or more, that'll throw up a big mud, but in that much water you can't be as precise with your casting. If you don't have good sun, you probably won't even see them. You'll be almost casting blind.

Ideal seeing conditions are, of course, experienced when the water isn't too deep in the middle of the day, eleven A.M. to two P.M., with the sun directly overhead, allowing you the best views of the bottom and minimizing the chances of scaring fish with shadows. In winter that is consistently the best time to fish. You can get them in the morning or evening, but seeing them will be a problem unless they're tailing. In the summer, however, the middle of the day may be too hot, so I am inclined to fish them early and late, from just after dawn to about eight A.M., then again about an hour before sunset, providing the tide is right.

In any case clear skies and good sunlight is always best and a pair of Polaroid sunglasses essential. Brown glasses, incidentally, seem to do the best job of cutting through the glare on the water. Cloudy days with limited vision can make for very tough fishing.

I like to fish the build to the moon, from medium low tide to medium high. I prefer a prevailing wind of less than ten miles an hour, just enough to ripple the surface. When the wind is steady and in the direction the fish are used to, they are steadier, too. Less skittish. At all times remember that the bonefish is very skittish, and you want to tackle him when there are as few reasons as possible for him to panic. Higher winds, by the way, are to your advantage in this regard. I frequently catch larger bonefish when the prevailing wind is fifteen to twenty miles an hour. With the more natural wave action on the surface, the fish seem more secure in their movements. You may not be able to see them as well, but they can't see you as well either, and when the surface is roiling, a lure splashing down is not as distracting.

Why fish from a skiff when you create a much lower and therefore less disturbing silhouette in waders? Mobility, for one thing. You can move around more freely in a small area in waders, but you can cover much more territory in a skiff. More importantly the bottom of a salt-water flat can be treacherous. In some places the mud and marl can suck you down. Some guys go on the flats barelegged, in old tennis shoes, but I wouldn't advise that either: you can pick up some nasty infections when scraping against coral or some of the undersea life that grows on flats, and there's always the chance you'll get stung by a man o' war. The best argument against wading, however, is that it limits your visibility.

The Angling

To be a good bonefisherman you have to be at least two things: one, you have to be as careful and stealthy as the bonefish is nervous and skittish or chances are you'll never get together, and two, you have to be extra careful handling and working your lure. The biggest mistake, the No. 1 error in bonefishing, is retrieving too fast. Unfortunately retrieving too slow is no advantage either.

Real bonefishing begins with the search for that good tidal flat already described; preferably you will do this at least once with a guide who knows the area and the fish. The considerations are not so complicated once you have the flat scouted.

Pole on from an angle where the current will work with you and ideally the sun won't throw shadows ahead of you. Pole as carefully as you can; do not let the pole strike the sides of the skiff. At the same time scan the flat for signs of fish feeding in the area. If you spook a bonefish or even a school in the process, stay calm and just go about your business. Unless you've really frightened them, they'll eventually come back or settle down.

Once on, look for tails breaking the water as the bonefish feed. They generally feed crosscurrent to pick up scents from the tide. If they're not tailing but moving slowly, they'll usually push wake ahead of them. Watch for dorsal fins slicing the surface. If you see nothing, look beneath the surface. Train your eyes to ignore the water and focus on the bottom. The practiced eye can pick up moving bonefish at surprising distances. On the bigger Bahamian flats bonefish sometimes feed in huge schools, two hundred fish or more; at other times there might only be four or five. Watch for shadows, for puffs of mud. At times, the experienced bonefisherman will look for mud more than he will fish.

Once you see something to make a move on, remember where you are. If the sun is at your back, you might have to crouch down a little.

I get on my knees to cast if I think my shadow will spook the fish, but that's not usually necessary. I frequently cast three-quarter arm, or even sidearm, to lessen the chances of making a moving shadow. A sidearm cast might not be as accurate, but it lays the lure on the surface a little more gently than an overhead cast, so it can be a double advantage.

Knowing that bonefish feed across the tide, you can position yourself properly to gauge their advance. If I haven't already done so, when I see fish I set the push pole in the mud and tie on. If the tide isn't moving enough to float me out of range, I might just lay the pole quietly in the boat and drift.

A lot of anglers believe bonefish require the most precise casting of all, and I wouldn't disagree. If you cast too far, they ignore you; too close, they scatter. Sometimes they react differently, depending on the day. Ordinarily a good cast with spinning tackle in two to three feet of water should put the lure three or four feet in front of the bonefish if he's tailing. His nose is in the mud, but he'll see that and turn on it. If he's already moving on to his next course, you have to be out ahead farther, varying the distance according to how fast he is swimming. You might want to be as much as ten feet in front.

When you get a feel for it, you'll frequently find it best to cast not only in front of the fish but on the other side of his advance as well, so that you angle the lure across his path and ahead of his nose. There are times, too, on a tailing bonefish when your only choice will be to cast directly behind him. That's not the most productive, but it can work.

If you're using a fly rod, make your false casts to the side, so there is less chance of a distraction. But don't be afraid to throw the fly right on top of a tailing bonefish. That's a departure from what some guides say, but I think it's better because the fly doesn't make that much of a splash and as soon as it hits you'll know if you've got the bonefish's attention. You risk spooking him, maybe, but chances are a well-presented fly will only turn his mind away from the crustaceans he's been after. If he's moving, gauge his speed and aim to land the fly in front of his nose. How far in front would depend on the depth he is swimming. In three feet of water I'd say put it six feet in front. In shallow water you might put it only two feet in front. Another big mistake anglers make bonefishing is casting too far in front.

Incidentally I don't use sinking line with flies because I like the luxury of being able to retrieve and immediately cast again. Too, you don't really need sinking line to get down the foot or so to the bottom of a bonefish flat. The advantage of a fly at that depth, besides making less splash on entry, is that it is less likely to catch on the bottom.

Bonefish move and feed more by smell than sight, and of course they put their snout right into the bottom to feed. If you're on a grass flat, you might want to let the lure drift, but keep it moving or it will hang up. On a rocky or sandy bottom some anglers let it lay as they wait for the fish, then twitch it to get their attention as they close in. The trouble is you can lose track of exactly where the lure is, and that can throw your timing off when starting your retrieve.

As I said, the biggest mistake anglers make is being too quick with the retrieve. Whether you're using a jig or a weighted fly, you follow a pattern: jump it (jerk the lure toward you) and then let it mud (settle to the bottom). Jump it and let it mud. Jump it, let it mud. Bump, bump, bump, at about five- to six-inch intervals. To the bonefish it will resemble a shrimp or a crab or a small crawfish trying to get away.

The bonefish is a slower feeder than the tarpon. When you see you've got him interested, speed up your retrieve—zip, zip, zip. With spinning make the lure jump without much forward movement by using a short up-and-down stroke. Some recommend these strokes be shorter, moving the lure not more than a couple of inches at a time. I prefer a little more flourish. When I use a fly, however, I go to a retrieving action, with strings of three to six inches. I might increase that when I have to get his attention from a greater distance, but I think you ought to be a little provocative with your retrieve when he's acting like he's ready to make his move. Wake him up. Get him eager.

That final little zip-zip-zip will do the job. When you give it that last small pause, stopping the lure, the bonefish can get his underslung mouth over the fly. He will then turn, either because he has taken it or because he has decided to pass. You try to feel it on the line by lifting your rod slightly. You have to be sure before you strike. If he hasn't got it, give it another brisk strip to regain his attention.

Another consideration of shadows and distractions has to do with the length of your cast. Always remember where you are in relationship to the movement of the fish. If you cast thirty feet to a moving bonefish, and he follows it ten feet, when he's about to hit he might only be twenty feet from the boat. Be as inconspicuous as possible. Always keep in mind how skittish he is.

That first contact with the hook is only a prelude to what the bonefish is really all about, so don't be confused. He won't take it like gangbusters right away; the explosion will come a couple of seconds later. He'll give it a nudge or make a turn, usually a sure sign he has it, then kind of walk off with it. Regardless of whether you're using spinning gear or a fly rod, you never strike him until either you feel him on or the line starts to go. When you feel him on, wait for the line to tighten, then whip your rod hard, raising it sharply to set the hook.

Then it's cowboys and Indians.

The realization that he is hooked will send the bonefish on a mad, reckless dash across the flat. You can't be too bold with him then because the smallest running bonefish can pop a line that tests twice its weight. I've known them to break line three times their weight. Remember, too, that he will be abetted by coral snags, mangrove shoots, crustaceans, any number of things that protrude from the flat to foul or break a line.

It would be nice to keep his nose up and your line out of trouble on that first run, but you have to be realistic. Line is screaming out. He's a hot fish; but he's also a running fish, not a jumping fish. Keep your rod high but the tip down—the less friction on the guides the better.

There is a second advantage to keeping the tip down: when he finally turns, you'll be ready to come up on him immediately without creating any slack. Give a self-respecting bonefish any kind of slack and he'll get a second wind or tangle your line. If he comes back hard against a belly in the line, he'll drag it across all those obstacles on the bottom and likely pop it or he'll slip the hook. Chances are the hook will set firmly in a bonefish. It plants well in that gristly mouth. You increase your odds all around by keeping a tight line.

I start with about a pound to a pound-and-a-half drag for bonefish

Handling a hooked bonefish—as delicately as possible.

and check it regularly as I'm fishing. When the fish is not so ripe, and I've got a good idea of its size, I sometimes increase the drag; but you judge this by the condition of the fish. An increased drag on a hot fish will leave you empty handed. When the fish is near the boat the only way I increase the drag is with a palm or thumb on the spool.

Be especially alert for slack when a bonefish is around the boat. He'll be in perpetual motion. If he runs toward the boat, keep your rod up and reel in hard. Don't let him create slack. Don't think in terms of turning a bonefish like a tarpon; think more of just keeping the pressure on. On his early runs he'll probably turn himself. He usually does that in order to stop and rub his nose on the bottom, trying to free himself from the hook and line. Of course if he is taking too much line too quickly, you have to turn him as soon as he stops. Never allow a standstill. Change the angle and turn him or increase the drag; but do not let him fight you to a standoff. To turn him, come up with the rod smoothly and carefully, slowing him down before the turn.

Bellies in the line can put a quick end to fishing on the flat because of all the obstacles under the surface. I am sure the fish is as aware of

Carefully removing the lure.

A moment in the boat for a picture, then a quick release.

that as you are. When he's around the boat, he'll start circling. He may go around four or five times before you have him near enough for the net. Again, don't worry about turning him. Just keep the rod pointed in the direction he's swimming. Invariably you'll be bringing him closer with each circle.

When you're going to net him, raise the tip of your rod as high as you can, to get him as near the surface as possible. At that point you should have no problems, but it is a critical time for the fish's survival. If you're not using a net, or if you're going to lift him out of the net, take him by the lower lip and tail, not by the gills. Poke around into his gills and you'll hurt him, maybe fatally.

If the bonefish seems sluggish after you've removed the hook, work him forward and backward just below the surface, forcing water through his gills. If he tends to go over on his side as you start to turn him loose, work him again the same way. A bonefish in a winded condition is easy prey for a barracuda or shark.

99

Atlantic salmon fishing at the moment of fulfillment. This 20-pound hen was caught and released on the Cains River in New Brunswick.

3

FISHING FOR ATLANTIC SALMON

The Experience
with Ted Williams

I didn't see him go over. It was more a matter of hearing it happen from a temporary limbo, as one might experience the emanations from a home run at the moment one has chosen to step down to the concession stand for a hot dog. In this case it was the shrill relaying of information from Edna, the housekeeper, from a vantage point (I could only imagine) near the window overlooking the river. There she often stands to look out, never more than a broom handle's length or two from her beloved skillets and double boilers. "Lord, God! Come quick! Ted's in the water!"

I was in the basement, suffering a communications gap with the long-distance operator. The telephone is at the bench where Ted ties his flies. Usually it is sequestered among the mounds of animal hair and tinsel strands that comprise the backbone of the wardrobe of his petite creations. As a concession to the outside world he will sometimes answer it there. Upstairs when he is preparing to fish or to eat or to sleep or to make entries in his log, he is more likely to give it the indifference he thinks it deserves. In the local Blackville directory the phone is listed under "Spaulding Trappers Association," or an equivalent, to further discourage intrusions.

I hung up on the operator, glad for the excuse, and bounded up the steps to the main floor of the cabin. Edna was now on the porch. Her apron was at her mouth. I banged through the screen door but had to pull up short to allow my eyes to adjust to the late afternoon glare off the Miramichi. Framed by the stand of white birch trees that surround the camp, the great glittering ribbon dominated an altogether lovely view. It is hard to think of the Miramichi as being a party to violence, but like all rivers it gets its share, and more than that now when the high incidence of salmon poaching has led to bloodshed.

103

Much of a dedicated salmon angler's time on the Miramichi is spent at his fly-tying bench. For Williams it is pure pleasure.

Watch on the river from Ted's camp window.

The Miramichi is the most productive salmon river in the hemisphere.

It is 100 feet, almost straight down, from his porch to the river. When I finally saw him, he was already out of the deeper water and trudging through the shallows, pulling the canoe behind him on a painter. In that Rockwellian perspective he looked like a large worn-out boy trailing home his sled after a day on the slopes.

We waited for him.

"You don't look so hot," I said as he reached the knoll at the top of the crude steps that lead up from the river.

"I'm all right," he said, wheezing.

He was not really all right. He was an obelisk of wet leather and rubber and soaked-through flannel, and the water squished in his waders. His breath came in audible bursts and made cartoonist balloons in the cold Canadian air. He sat down heavily on the wooden bench and began to remove his waders.

"Roy says you're a cow in a canoe."

"There's a lot of jealousy around here," he said. "A lot of jealousy."

"What happened?"

"The water's high and I wanted to fish a spot on the other side. I was standing up poling across, and the pole got pinched against the middle of the canoe by the current. Alluva sudden I was over."

I had a flash image of a grim scenario: of the pole banging into his head, of the canoe smothering him, of his waders filling with water and tugging him down, of the river rushing over him. Canoe Flips; Hall-of-Famer Washed Into Oblivion.

"You better get right in and take a warm bath and get some dry clothes on," Edna said, her practical jaw set. She was looking at him sternly. "You'll catch your death."

"No time to shower. I'm gonna change and go back," he said, and abruptly stood up and lumbered through the door. I watched the screen tremble and looked at Edna. She rolled her eyes.

"He'd do that?" I asked. "He'd go back now, cold as it is, after almost drowning?"

"It's still light, ain't it?" said Edna, and went inside. She had, after all, said her piece.

Roy Curtis, Edna's husband and Ted's guide, came after that. He had been off in the pickup on an errand and was back to fetch Edna home just as Ted retraced the steps to the river in dry clothes and waders. Told of the near catastrophe, Roy joined me on the porch to watch, both of us now well jacketed against the evening's advance. He said they had already fished a full day without luck at another place, and after Edna had filled them with the usual surfeit of calories, Ted had announced his intentions to salvage something here, at the home pool.

The Curtises have been in his employ since the late 1950's. They bestow on him a tender but cautious devotion, not so much out of his celebrity (that they merely tolerate) but because of his uniqueness. He brings to their lives a security in a wretchedly insecure world—one third the citizens of New Brunswick are on relief in the winter—and the uneasy excitement parents might feel in rearing a generous but temperamental prodigy. In turn they take care that all his needs on the river are met. The porch where we stood was built by Roy; he had in fact helped build all three cabins in the camp. In the fishing season he also guides the visitors Ted favors with invitations to the camp. In the winter he makes repairs and sees to the cutting of wood for the Franklin stove.

I asked Roy if he remembered the first time they had fished together, and he said yes, in 1955 "when we were both young fellers." Roy is a stockily built man, sixtyish, with cloudy blue eyes and cheeks

A long time "unbeatable" team: Roy Curtis and Ted Williams on the Mirami-chi River.

that glow like slabs of country ham. Taciturn, he makes the perfect fishing companion for a fishing genius. That and the fact that he is highly respected for his expertise among the salmon guides of the province makes him special to Ted. The evaluations Ted seeks in fishing matters could not be given by sycophants.

"He asked me if I knew anything about salmon fishing," Roy said.

"What did you tell him?"

"I said, 'Some.' "

"He was pretty cocky, uh?"

"No. Well, yes. Maybe a little. But in forty years on the river I've met an awful lot of fishermen; and most of 'em, either they can't fish a' tall or after a year or so they start telling *you*. Most of 'em you have to straighten out for sure."

"You had to straighten Ted out?"

107

He grinned, "Some. But don't tell him I told you that. The thing is, I liked him right off. He's such a great big kid, you know. Just a dandy fellow to be with. And, of course, now I really can't tell him anything. He likes to tell me."

"I think he believes he's the best," I said. "Is he the best?"

"The best I've seen," said Roy. "Forty years, and I ain't seen none better, no. There's days a feller can beat him, maybe, but day in, day out, he's the best. He can do it all. He can tie the best flies, rig 'em just right. He can cast to the toughest spots. He can cover more water than anybody. He knows exactly how to play 'em, and he has a fine steady hand to release 'em, and that's an art for sure. Sometimes I sit on the bank and never lift a finger."

"I bet you like that."

Roy ignored me. "And *persistent*, oh, my. He'll stay out there all day, any kind of weather. Stay and stay. Another feller'd quit, but he won't. He has wonderful staying power."

He nodded at the Miramichi, and we watched from our perch. Ted was alone now, moving along the near side of the silver gash, casting, moving a step or two downriver, casting, moving. Edna brought us Scotch to warm the vigil. The silence between us grew as we watched. Then, when it was almost impossible to see, there was a small detonation on the surface of the water, a flash of tumbling flesh, and a quick, one-sided battle. The lone figure moved to the river's edge, his rod held high in one hand, his other reaching down as he bent over.

"He's releasing it?" I asked.

"Yeah," said Roy.

"All day for one fish, and he's releasing it?"

"Yeah," said Roy Curtis. "Persistent."

A stunning rendition of reveille, full and reedy and unorthodox, stirred the camp at first light. Ted stood in the open area between the main house and the guest cabin. He had his heels together and his backbone arched, and he let his splendid stomach thrust forward unchecked. With his forefinger and thumb curled and pressed hard to his mouth to form a facsimile bugle, he blew again, toward the river, this time the Marine Hymn ("From the halls of Montezuma . . ."). As a former Marine fighter pilot he finds it applicable to almost any situation—a call to dinner, a salute to a passing duck, a response to a smart-aleck remark.

The second burst drew a shout and a wave from a bulky gray silhouette on the Miramichi. A single fisherman had already established his position ahead of the inevitable crowd. Ted watched the angler cast and from that could name him. "He was in my pool again yesterday in his canoe," he said to Roy Curtis. "I'm gonna have to have him over for a drink so I can tell him he's fishing right over the hot spot." He said he didn't mind the natives fishing his pools, but "you'd think a licensed angler would have the courtesy to ask."

"Maybe you're jealous that he can handle a canoe," I said.

"Maybe you don't know how lucky you are to be here," he said, lifting the side of his mouth.

He walked to the truck where Roy was loading waders and extra rain gear. During the night, great black sheets of rain had slashed into the camp, and there was threat of more. He said I was about to join the "best fishing team on the Miramichi," Williams and Curtis, and that it would do me well to pay attention. "We could make history today," he said.

Edna came out with lunch in a bulging brown bag, and Roy slipped it into his backpack. We piled into the pickup, Roy at the wheel, Ted at the other window. They had decided to try his pool at Grey Rapids, downriver toward Newcastle. The pool washes into a long stretch of rocky, active public water and makes a first-rate salmon run. By canoe it is no more than two miles from his camp, but it is a half-hour drive by truck. We circled back the four miles to Blackville, crossed over onto Route 8, and then picked our way down a series of unpaved side roads.

"Why not just use the canoe?" I asked.

It wasn't done, he said. "And that kind of fishing holds no fascination for me. They use canoes a lot on the Restigouche, but I don't like it. You can't make subtle moves in a canoe. You can't get right down there with 'em, where it's intimate." He raised his eyebrows.

On the side roads we passed knots of school children, waiting at unmarked bus stops in the gray light. Brightly clad and scrubbed-looking, they stood out like bouquets against the beaten-looking houses and farms. Ted waved and called to those he knew. At the property line of one larger spread he leaned out the window and began yelping and banging on the door. "Yip! Yip! Yip!" We were almost to the fence on the other side of the property when a large German shepherd suddenly shot out from its hiding place behind a bush and ran toward us, barking ominously. At the fence the big dog pulled up short but continued to bark. Ted responded, holding up his end of the duet. "Yip! Yip! Yip!"

Ted and Roy laughed happily. "Bastard does it every time," Ted said.

Ted remembers "everything" about every salmon catch. Note the rod position as he plays this one with guide Hud Minor. The 14-pounder was caught and released at Swinging Bridge on the Miramichi.

We turned down a dirt road, creased and pocked by the drastic New Brunswick winters and now made treacherous by the rain. Roy grunted as he worked the gears, the pickup hammering and pawing along, gaining and losing and regaining traction.

Ted said that that first time on the Miramichi, when he was still playing for the Red Sox, had not exactly thrilled him. He had come up to do a fishing film. The script called for him to span seasonal lines to go for bass, bonefish, tarpon, and salmon, and it had been a job getting it all in. "You couldn't even think about that now, of course," he said. "They've made the baseball season too damn long for that. Too long, period. It's lousy for baseball. Lousy. Cold, rotten weather at the beginning of the season, cold, rotten weather at the end. I'd be screaming if I played now. I *hated* to hit in cold weather. They wanta know why batting averages are so low, that's a factor."

He said he was not immediately won to the salmon. "In the first place I didn't like standing in line on the river with five guys in front of you and five guys behind you, and guys casting right across from you, sometimes close enough to hit you in the eye. I didn't like having to fish somebody's private pool. It was a good pool, but I didn't like that part of the act.

"Then a guy gave me a couple flies he'd tied that were half the size of the ones I was using, and I got some fish, and I thought, 'Gee, if I could tie my own flies, and if I had my own pool. . . .' Eventually I got a pool, too, and right away came the biggest flood in fifty years and moved the rocks around and wrecked the whole damn thing."

By 1958, he said, he was hooked. That year he won his last American League batting championship, a steal at .328 compared with his supernal .388 of the year before. As one Williamsphile observed at the time, he had at least proved he was the greatest old hitter who ever lived. In 1958 he turned forty. Right after the last game he flew to Bangor, Maine, picked up his friend Bud Leavitt of the Bangor *News* and drove straight through to the Miramichi. They were on the river the next afternoon, beating the close of the salmon season by just two hours.

"It was cold as hell, and the wind was ripping down the river," he said. "I had to fish on the left side to keep the fly away from me—a tough day to cast. But I'd been tying flies all summer, and I had a yellow butt on a double three with a short shank, and I laid it out there. And I kept laying it out there—picking up slowly, laying it out. I didn't see a fish. Then there was a big boil, and I put it out again, and there was that beautiful roll and the feel of weight that you get when

A good salmon is always worth smiling about.

he's taken the fly. *Whooosh.* He was way downriver before he jumped, and I could see him for the first time. Then he came back upriver and greyhounded right past me. He fought like hell for about thirty minutes. A twenty-pound hookbill, the best I ever got on the river. A guy across the way saw the whole thing and came over. He said, 'I heard what a helluva fisherman you were, and I wanta tell you, you are a helluva fisherman.' He had a camera. If it wasn't for that I wouldn't have a record of it."

"Over twenty years ago and you can remember that?"

"Like it was yesterday. You remember everything that happens about a salmon. You forget about the others but not the salmon."

Two trucks were already parked in the clearing that bordered on the narrow trail to the river.

"It'll be crowded today," Ted said, hurrying to put on his waders. "The Miramichi fishes ten times more anglers than any other salmon river, wouldn't you say, Roy?"

"For sure," said Curtis. He and I were still gathering up equipment when Ted plunged through the opening in the bushes toward the river, rod in hand. When we reached the bank, he was rigged and moving into the water. His pool was farther up and around the bend from where we came out, Roy said. This was public water through to the bottom end of the rapids. Three men were already on the river, casting.

I waited on the bank as Roy deposited our gear. I wasn't eager to fish too close to Ted's scrutiny. Too, my own insecurities about fly casting were giving me rookie jitters. I had done little, none in years. Ted stripped out line and began to cast, the fluid ease and enormous power that made him so marvelous a hitting specimen reborn. The wind was angling into us; he double hauled to build up line speed and cast again. The line shot forward with a sharp whistling sound and at its full length sent the tippet rolling out like a lizard's tongue to flick the water, delicately laying on the fly. An eighty-foot cast. Farther out a zipper on the surface signaled a fish. His next cast covered the distance.

"See that?" said Roy. "He *drives* it out there. He's got a bull arm. That's one reason he gets more 'n anybody. He reaches 'em where the ordinary fellow can't."

Roy pointed down and across the river to a crude log cabin high on the bank. He said he was born there. He said one windy fall morning a few seasons ago he had come across from that point in a canoe and spotted a big salmon lying by a submerged rock. "When we fished that day we couldn't get anything, and I finally said to Ted, 'The waves is high, and the wind is right on you, but if you can get it out there, there's a dandy big salmon. I can't reach it, but I can tell you when you're over it.' The wind was in his face and the waves was pullin' his line over every time he cast, but finally he got it right there, and I said, 'That's it.' And he kept casting. He stood there for two hours casting. And do you know he nailed that fish? A fifteen-pounder. The only fish caught that day."

"That was a holding fish," Ted said. He had come back to change flies and make an adjustment on his leader. The light had changed, he said, and with the higher water he needed something brighter. "A fish that's holding will take ten times better than a fish that's running."

From the pocket of his flannel shirt he took out and opened what resembled a metal cigarette case. Inside in neat little rows, like earrings in a jeweler's display, were the flies he had been tying at night in the basement.

Just being there, hard beside a salmon stream, can make a contented man.

Experimenting with and studying the action of a new rod.

There are many reasons to concentrate on a cast.

"You know, Roy," he said, "I discovered something about tying a Conrad a couple days ago, and I think you oughta know—something that could help you a lot." But instead of showing Roy the fly, he cupped his hand over the case mysteriously.

Roy grinned and waited.

"Naw, I better not," Ted said. "I better keep this to myself. You're a big Canadian guide, up all night tying flies. These amateur efforts wouldn't interest you." He turned and held the fly out of sight, studying it. "I don't know if you're ready for this or not."

Roy waited. Finally, inevitably, Ted turned back to reveal his creation. Roy adjusted his glasses and held the fly up to the morning light.

"Yeah, that's a good one," he said.

"A good one? A good one? Boy, there *is* a lot of jealousy around here. That's a peppermint stick, that fly. Even you could catch fish with that fly. I was gonna make you a little presentation, too, but now . "

"Oh, I'll take it for sure," said Roy.

"Yeah, yeah, I knew you'd say that." Ted winked at me. "What do you think of Ted Williams now? What - do - you - think - of - Ted - Williams?"

When he was rerigged, he moved upriver, around the bend to his own pool, and out of sight. Roy took me out to join the line of fishermen in the public water. One of them, farther down, raised a fish and then lost it. Roy grunted.

"I like to see that," he said. "I want a fisherman to get his salmon, for sure; but just the same I still root for the salmon. That one'll be that much harder to get next time. Might be he'll educate his children. Might be he'll tell his sons, 'Don't get near that thing, because I had an experience one time.' "

A fly box full of Williams'
homemade delicacies.

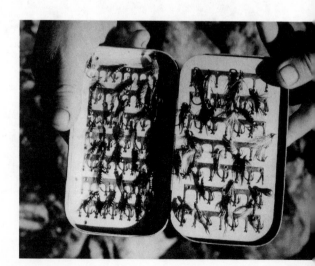

Satisfied that he had established a moral, Roy left me and went back to rig for himself. The conga line had increased in number until we were now nine. Like polyps on a vine we moved downriver, maintaining our intervals. At a point where the river widened and deepened, the procession ended and in turn we walked back to start over. When I looked upriver, I saw Ted was at the bend, hunched over near the shoreline, apparently releasing a fish. He moved back into the river and began casting again.

I finished the run and waited on a rock.

"A salmon?" I asked when he came.

"The one I released? A grilse, four to five pounds tops."

I said no one else caught anything.

"I know," he said. He was repairing his line, cutting the leader with his teeth. "This is one fish you have to be satisfied with one a day. A good-sized tarpon, fifty pounds or so, you'd be satisfied with one. An eight- or nine-pound bonefish, you'd be tickled to death with one. A nice day. But this one, you don't even think so much about size." He said there was "no question thirty- and forty-pounders come up this river, but they're rare, and they're more likely to come late in the fall, past the season. You'd be lucky even to see one. On the Restigouche a thirty-pounder is not unusual. Up there getting a thirty-pounder would be like the year I hit .400 [actually .406 in 1941]. There were guys who hit .340, .359 that year, so hitting .400 wasn't such a big deal at the time. Now, when the best hitters in the big leagues are hitting .310, .400 would be a hell of a big deal."

Almost simultaneously, not five feet apart and less than ten yards away, two fish jumped. Tempted, Ted moved back into the river and began casting. I waited until he was a safe distance, then fell in line. We followed the queue twice more, working from the top of the pool to the bottom. Every now and then I caught his gaze, checking me out. Invariably at those times I sent up erratic casts. Once, trying for distance, I hooked my hat on the follow through, and he saw that, too. He said it was all right, that he still did it occasionally. "That's why I always wear a hat," he said. "Otherwise you're picking it out of your ear."

Lunchtime drew together a circle of fishermen at the bank where Roy had laid our gear. Roy sat on a rock and peeled the waxed paper from Edna's salmon salad sandwiches. The other anglers clustered around, waiting for Ted, who was the last to leave the river. Except for the one near miss and the grilse I had seen Ted release, there hadn't been a pull.

Underwood waits his turn on the Miramichi.

"There's fish," Ted said, attacking his sandwich. "They're just not taking, that's all. That one refuse the bug, Leo, or what?"

"Yeah," said the man who missed the fish. He seemed surprised Ted had seen it, having been at least a quarter mile away at the time.

"Geez, and you one of the all-time greats," Ted needled.

"Water's way up," said an older man in a baggy shirt. His face showed the unmistakable folds of a drastic weight loss. "Must be swollen six inches since last night."

"Oh, hell yes," said Williams. "This could be a total loss today. Real dirty water, coming fast. We probably oughta try Swinging Bridge tomorrow, Roy."

"I'd say," said Roy.

"You don't like rising water, Ted?" Leo said.

"At the beginning of a rise, yes. Ordinarily I like high water because the fish come in then, as opposed to a draft when there's no water for them to move in. But when it's discolored like this, it's a signal for them to move on."

"What do you mean, 'move on'?" I asked.

120

"They don't hold in the pools as well. They see their chance and move. Still, there are pools in June and early July, high water pools, that are good to fish in. How fast the water moves is a factor. I use bigger flies in June, when it's moving, and smaller flies in low water and during the summer when the water is slow. When it's really hot in July, they don't even like to come up. They wait down in the bay for cooler water."

"What moon do you like?" the old man asked.

"The build of the moon is the best. They'll move in that water all night. They travel the least from about ten A.M. to four P.M."

"Why do you suppose they take flies?" A younger man in a red hat and red suspenders, an American, had jumped into the discussion.

"Well, no one's sure. It's not out of hunger, though, I'm convinced of that. When they come up in the fall, they don't eat in the river at all. You ever found one that had anything in its belly going upriver, Roy?"

"Never did."

"Roy has opened thousands of fish, and he never found anything. Their bellies are just flat. Some guys say they go for bugs to squeeze the juice out of 'em, but that's crap. When they come upriver, they're here on business. To spawn, not to eat. In the spring it's a different story. They haven't eaten for five or six months, they're hungry, they're getting ready to go out. But I still think hitting the fly is more an instinctive thing. As parr [young salmon], they reacted to flies and bugs—they're voracious eaters. They eat anything that floats. One of the prettiest sights on the river is on a quiet summer evening when the bugs are hatching, and you can watch the salmon jump eight, ten, twelve inches to grab 'em. So they react to flies and bugs—a nervous stimulus, something that carried them in the beginning. Instinct. That, and the annoyance of having something enter their territory."

The man in the baggy shirt picked up Ted's rod.

"That's a lot bigger rod than I use, Ted. Gotta be a weightlifter to use that damn rod."

"Eight and a half feet, that's all," said Ted. He got up to demonstrate, putting his sandwich on the backpack. "Look, you're casting into the wind out here now, and it's ridiculous to use that little baton you're using—what is it, six and a half feet? I thought so. You might as well throw the fly with your hand. Adequate tackle. You've got to have adequate tackle, it's the first rule in the book, no matter what you're fishing for. All you do with inadequate equipment is frustrate yourself and maybe injure a fish that breaks off or stick a hook in your ear or in your eye. I was at a banquet twenty years ago, sitting next to a guy with a patch over one eye. He said he'd been an ambassador to Ireland, and he fished there and used a lighter rod, and when he tried to pick up the fly, it came back and hit him in the eye."

He worked the rod. "On a real windy day, I've used a nine-foot rod, with big flies. But eight and a half is all you need, nine in the toughest weather."

"But you're a lot bigger."

Ted gave him a look. "Yeah, and my eyesight is better, too, and all that other crap I'm supposed to have going for me. But what you really have to have out here, Bush, is talent. That's what it takes. A little bit of talent." He grinned, then made a face as the American in the red hat lit a cigarette.

"There was some guy on the other side smoking when I was fishing upriver," Ted said, talking to the group but looking at the smoker. "I could smell it all the way across. I could *smell* it. I know guys who'd commit adultery before they'd smoke one of those things."

The smoker grinned sheepishly. The others laughed.

A squat, dark-tanned man with a face like a clenched fist had been listening without expression. He kept glancing downriver. Finally a lone fisherman could be seen plowing through the shallows.

"My friend, he got a roll before," the man said in a thick French accent. He sighed. "We'll be here till five o'clock now. We were here to almost ten last night."

Ted took two donuts out of the bag and offered the Frenchman one.

"Sounds like my kinda guy," he said, and bit into his donut. "I went eight days without a roll or a pull one year after they started allowing the mackerel netting in the Miramichi Bay."

"I thought mackerel netting was always legal."

"It was. I'm talking about mackerel netting that wasn't mackerel netting at all. Salmon netting in disguise."

"The incidental catch, what a joke that is," said the man in the baggy shirt. "They catch ten legitimate mackerel and ninety incidental salmon, and they keep the salmon and throw away the mackerel."

"I didn't think any kind of commercial salmon netting on the river or in the bay was legal," I said.

"They banned it in 1972, when they realized this fish was in serious trouble and the Danes were murdering 'em off Greenland and on the high seas," said Ted. "In those days you saw very few commercial fishermen dropping nets for mackerel, only salmon. Then they put the ban on. The next thing you know they were selling mackerel licenses like crazy."

"They went from ninety nets to six hundred in no time," said the old man. "The salmon didn't know the difference. And the government allowed it."

"They've made some strides," said Ted. "They got limits now, and since 1980 they make you tag every fish that's sold, and that's good. And they forced the Danes to limit their netting on the high seas. But they gotta do more. I think it should be classified as a game fish and not a commercial fish. I know Jack Fenety doesn't agree with me on that, he doesn't think it's necessary yet, and we don't usually disagree, but I think it's essential."

"Who's Jack Fenety?" I asked.

"President of the Miramichi Salmon Association, and a helluva caring guy. He thinks the salmon oughta be a shared resource. But it's been proven over and over again, if you don't protect popular game that is also a resource, it goes. There just aren't enough salmon to go around—to the angler, to a guy who wants to net, to the commercial fisherman, to everybody. The main consideration should be how can we get the most revenue from this fish if it is in limited supply? And it is.

"People who think there is fishing for everybody are mistaken because that's what they thought about the prairie chicken and the ducks and the buffalo. The market can stand just so much. Game that's not here anymore is gone or going because too many people are after it. You have to consider what you're getting back from the people who take it, and you have to make up your mind in a hurry. For Ted Williams, who loves this fish, it's fast coming to the point where there won't be enough fishing to warrant the time and expense."

"They say more fish were caught on the rivers in this system last year than any in the past ten," said the man in the red hat. He was now cupping his cigarette in his hand but hadn't been intimidated enough to put it out.

"Yeah, they're making a big deal out of that now because the commercial fishermen want the ban lifted. But like Fenety says, one swallow doesn't make a summer, and one good year doesn't reverse a trend. The water was up and down, up and down, fresh all the time. They gotta give it three or four years, *ten* years before they can say a trend is set. It's still a long way from what it used to be."

"Will they get the ban lifted?"

"Looks that way, on a select basis. They're talking about a quota of eighteen thousand fish for commercial fishermen on the Miramichi [now in effect]. But they're also going to allow a legal catch of fourteen thousand fish plus the incidental catch in the Bay of Chaleur and in the Bay of Fundy. And in the end it's going to be screwed up as bad as it was in 1972. I think it's wrong."

"How about the Indians? They got carte blanche to net 'em, and they sell 'em, too."

"They say they don't, but you go into the reservations with a few bucks in your pocket and you can buy all you want," said the Frenchman.

"Well, I'll tell you," said Ted. "The poaching is wrong, no matter if it's the Indians doing it or the natives, but at least it's against the law. Commercial fishing will be legal and it'll set the river back ten years. They'll abuse it, abuse it, abuse it. There'll be just as much poaching, and then the Danes'll say, 'What the hell,' and they'll be netting 'em like crazy again, and that'll be the end of the salmon. And when they go, I go with 'em. Goodbye. See you later."

The old man said the commercial ban had gradually made the anglers the enemies of the locals. He said he had experienced their resentment: ice picks through his tires, holes knocked in his boat.

"Yeah," Ted said, "but hell, you have to give these people some consideration. They've fished this river all their lives. Most of us who have pools make some kind of allowance. I had one native tell me the other day, the greatest thing I ever heard. He said, 'All I live for now is this river. To be able to come here and fish.' I have sympathy for that kind of feeling."

"Do you have sympathy for burning out your camp when you're not here?" said the man in the baggy shirt. He said it had happened twice to friends of his, and they'd sold out and gone back to the States.

"They think we're infringing on their birthright, their right to take as many fish as they please," said Leo.

"That's what they said about the buffalo," Ted said. "Let 'em take whatever they want and what'll they have to show for it in the end?"

"Five bucks a pound on the black market."

"Yeah, well, I figured out what they'd be losing in my case," said Ted. "For every salmon I catch, I put two hundred dollars into the economy. In license fees, guides, taxes, equipment, supplies. I do it because I love this fish and feel lucky to have the chance to fish for it. I say that only to show you what an angler is worth to the economy of this province."

Catching the sunset on the rivers of New Brunswick. The fishing is almost secondary.

An increasingly rare experience in salmon fishing: a double.

One of the circle noted that a story in a local paper had quoted a confessed poacher as being critical of the duplicity of visiting sportsmen. He had singled out Williams himself for complaining about getting "only fifty-eight" salmon one year when the year before he had "over a hundred at the same time."

"Yeah, I saw that," said Ted, "and it's about what you'd expect from a newspaper. What I catch and what I release are two different things."

"For every ten you catch, how many do you keep?" the old man asked.

"Less than two," Ted said.

The others whistled.

"How many times you think you've cast for salmon in these waters?"

"You mean how many casts altogether? Well, I figure it takes three hundred casts to get a fish, and I've caught a thousand-plus. That's three hundred thousand casts at least."

More whistles.

"What's the most you ever caught in a season?"

"A hundred thirty-eight in 1967," Ted said. "And it's been downhill ever since."

We were back to camp before dark. After lunch Ted had caught and released a ten-pound hen, closing out his allowable fishing for the day. I slipped on a rock working downstream and swamped my waders, but in my misery I chanced on a grilse and landed it, and that warmed me some. Otherwise the activity at Grey Rapids was dispiriting, and when the clouds thickened and the cold came on again, we left the Frenchman to fish alone with his dogged friend.

Two men were waiting in the driveway when we rolled in, an old man with hair white as tissue and a middle-aged man with a big twitching smile that made you think bugs were loose under his skin. They identified themselves as devout Red Sox fans, a father-son team. The smiling man had a book for Ted to autograph.

Ted invited them to sit on the porch, and the white-haired man watched tentatively as the smiling man gushed over his hero.

"You could still play," the smiling man said.

"Play what? The piano?"

"No, I mean as a designated hitter," said the smiling man. "With those eyes, those wrists." He looked at me for approval. He couldn't stop grinning.

"Well, it takes more than eyes," said Ted.

"Oh, yes, I know. Yeah. I remember the way you gripped the bat. You always gave it that extra little twist before you hit. All that power."

"You remember that, eh?" Ted said. "Boy, one of my loyal fans."

The smiling man blushed happily, a baseball archeologist on a hot streak, digging up remembrances. "And the milk shakes. You drank a lot of milk shakes," he said.

"Is that what caused that gut?" I asked.

Ted raised the side of his mouth at me. "Boy, down the totem pole you go," he said. "Right out of the top ten on my list of friends, maybe never to return."

"Bob Feller says you were the best," the smiling man said. "I read it in the paper. He says the days of the super hitters are over—DiMaggio, Williams, Musial, Mays, Aaron. They don't make 'em like that no more."

Ted ignored the compliment. "Your dad's being awfully quiet," he said. "Must be a Mantle fan."

"No. Ruth and Gehrig," said the white-haired man softly.

"Well, at least somebody here has some class," Ted said, giving me a look.

After dinner, on the preparation of which he advised Edna extensively, he turned on the radio to pick up the Red Sox game and then settled on the sofa in front of the Franklin stove to write in his log. Scrapbook size, the log represents an ongoing investigation, filled with daily episodes and details, water and weather and so forth, on his salmon catches. On the first page he had written, "I start this book with seven-hundred-plus salmon and feel I know one hell of a lot about them and may be—there's no doubt in my mind about this— one of the greatest salmon anglers."

There were notes about the flies he had used ("I feel that the Conrad is absolutely the best"), the friends he had fished with ("So-and-so arrived and without a doubt is the worst fisherman I know"), the fish he had released ("I hope she makes it to the spawning grounds"), and about the good fortune of his fellow man ("Guy across the river caught two. He was either good or lucky. Strongly suspect latter").

A Reggie Jackson home run strained his interest in the game, and he was about to repair to the basement to tie flies when a man and a boy in khaki clothes knocked on the door. The man was a game warden, Percy Mountain, the boy his son. By his own description Mountain is a former poacher and "hard drinker" who had "gone to the other side," giving up both pleasures at the same time—roughly when he came to the conclusion that the beloved salmon was going under. Slightly built and wiry, he was obviously someone Ted liked and was welcomed in immediately.

Percy said he was on night patrol, hunting poachers in his motor-driven canoe. He said each year it got worse. He said there were now thirty wardens, carrying guns, covering the 400 miles of the Miramichi system, but it was a losing battle. He said the wardens were still five years behind the poachers, even in technology. They only got walkie-talkies after the poachers had them.

Unemployment was a factor in the increase in poaching, Percy said. He said the more people there were out of work, the more poaching there was. He said one night he pulled up nineteen nets, some of them stretching the width of the river. "It's cops and robbers out there," he said. Wardens had been shot and beaten with gas lanterns, sometimes by relatives. One warden had lost an eye. "I've had enough rocks thrown at me to fill this room," he said.

"Emery Bastrache [a former conservation officer] was stoned on the head one night," Ted said. "I put it in the log: 'I wonder when they're going to wake up and give these guys the authority they need.'"

Percy said they were making some progress. That one poacher had been fined $1,500 and had his truck and fishing gear confiscated. But with salmon bringing $5 a pound on the black market, "a good poacher can make enough in one night to pay the usual fine."

"You need some PR," said Ted. "Educate everybody—the schools, the kids, everybody—on how important this fish is to the province. How poaching is going to ruin it for everybody."

Percy said the poachers had beaten them to it. One had gone right on TV, saying he'd kill any warden who got in his way. "He's on welfare, too," he said. "The government supports him."

"How easy is it?" I asked. "To poach, I mean."

"I could do it blindfolded every night and never get caught," Percy said.

There is no bridge at Swinging Bridge Pool, only the remains of one—the fossil of an abutment that helps form a small island at the bottom end of Ted's pool and another abutment on the far side of the Miramichi. Cables once supported a footbridge. A heavy ice jam knocked out the footbridge in 1970, and there had been no attempt to replace it. The pool, fourteen miles upriver from the main camp, is

200 yards long, with a gravel bar that makes a kind of spinal column that the fish must pass over. It is Ted's favorite, good enough to have accounted, he estimates, for half the salmon he has caught on the Miramichi.

We were joined there by a fellow member of the Miramichi Salmon Association, a friend from Bathurst named Alex Fekeshazy. Fekeshazy is a burly bearlike man with a clement personality whose fishing outfits are not complete without a Save the Atlantic Salmon button pinned on somewhere.

The storm had passed, and the weather improved. Ted was in high spirits. He showed Fekeshazy a fly he had tied the night before, a green-butt version of the Conrad with silver tinsel, ribbed bear hair, and green florescent floss.

"Oh baby, that one will catch fish," Ted said. "With that one it could happen."

He grinned and tied it deftly to the leader. "I should'a' been a surgeon," he said.

The prevailing wind comes downriver at Swinging Bridge. Ted cast high, letting the wind carry the payload. "See that?" he said. "An easy eighty-foot cast."

I was on a nearby boulder, sitting it out for a while. He obliged me with a blow-by-blow.

"My first act now, when it's straight out and downstream like that, is a slight move up with the rod, just in case a salmon hits. Just a slight five- to ten-degree bend. Now, there, see how the fly is swimming? The water's faster now. The slacker the water, the more bend I put in the rod to encourage the lure to swim faster. Speed of the fly is very important."

He reeled in and cast again.

"Yeah, we'll see fish today," he said to Fekeshazy. "This is a good holding pool. There'll be fish today."

As if in response, stitches began to appear on the water in front of him, evidence of salmon rolling.

He worked downriver, casting. I had turned toward the shore to get my gear when I looked back and saw him walking toward the bank, his line taut.

"Geez," he called. "I got bottom."

The ingredients of a catch: playing and landing an Atlantic salmon. Ted uses the bend of the rod as cushion, working his left hand for leverage and control. At the finish, he hoists a 14-pounder.

The fish he had hooked made a spectacular somersault cross-river. Ted grinned.

He never wasted a motion. When the fish jumped, he instinctively leaned to it. When it ran, he waited for the moment it tired, then deftly turned it. When he had it flopping in the shallows, Roy scooped the net under it and hauled it out. A fifteen-pound hookbill. This one, he said, they would have to take home for the pot.

"What do you think of Ted Williams?" Ted said, as Roy lifted the catch from the net and held it up by the tail. Roy finished the kill and laid it under a blanket of river grass for safekeeping. Ted curled his finger and thumb and pressed them against his lips and sent a chorus of the Marine Hymn keening downriver.

The Expertise:
Ted Williams on Atlantic Salmon

The Fish—and Where to Catch It

For anybody to select a big three of anything requires at least a little prejudice. To choose a No. 1 requires more. But after half a century of fishing, for just about everything that swims and in just about every kind and body of water, I am convinced that the Atlantic salmon is the greatest of game fish. There's nothing that can touch it for all-around enjoyment. If that's a personal prejudice, I'm in good company. I know a lot of guys who feel the same way.

What are the requirements of a good fish? Size is a criterion, but it can't stand alone. I've caught a 1,000-pound white marlin, and I wouldn't really care to catch another. I've caught 400- and 500-pound tuna, and big blue marlin and scores of sailfish. I've caught a 600-pound thresher shark. You might as well call a thresher shark a Mack truck, because that's the way it fights.

Fighting ability is a better criterion. The tarpon is a more spectacular fighting fish, an eager, tackle-busting fish that bends hooks and breaks lines. The salmon doesn't always fight like that, but he fights. No fish makes a more impressive first run than a bonefish. The salmon doesn't always run like that, but he *runs.* I've had twelve-pound salmon that would run as long as any twelve-pound bonefish and jump as much as any tarpon and take me a quarter mile downstream doing it.

Then there are all the other factors. Where you catch them, how you catch them, the skill involved. You catch salmon in beautiful surroundings, places you never get tired of going to. There's constant expectation. You're always seeing fish, seeing them jump, seeing them roll, seeing them walk over a bar. The technique you have to have for salmon is awesome. Sometimes they're so hard to take you think

133

A beautiful 15-pounder, caught at Swinging Bridge.

they're smart, and sometimes it's just a matter of changing the angle of your cast a little bit. And you have to consider all the tackle you can use—the flies you can tie, wet or dry, and the fun of that. The fun of having a fish roll on a fly. And the added pleasure of the salmon being extremely edible. Most game fish you can't eat at all.

And, gee, the Atlantic salmon is such a romantic fish. The life cycle is so romantic. They know specifically that a salmon hatched up the Miramichi River in New Brunswick, fifty miles or more, will stay in the river three years, surviving kingfishers, eels, skunks, mergansers, coons, otters, everything in the river that takes shots at him. Then the third summer he runs the gauntlet to the sea. Man's after him, beast's after him; but he goes out, no one knows where for sure, and he survives the predators there and the ocean netters, and finally a year later he comes back upriver a grilse (a small adult salmon), maybe four or five pounds, right back to the exact same area he was spawned. Or, if he has the appropriate genes, he might wait another year and come back a nine-pound to a twelve-pound salmon. At that point he's a 4,000 to 1 shot. The hen that went upriver four or five years before laid around 8,000 eggs. They figure the best you can hope for is that two salmon will survive everything and make it back four years later.

The tarpon's a super fish, and the bonefish is a super fish. You never quite get your bellyful of those two. But *this* fish. It keeps getting on you, more and more. You dream about 'em. You think about the next time, the ways you'll fish for them. The flies you'll use. The different pools, the hot spots in the pools, the tricks to get in position when they show themselves or come to the fly.

All the great fishermen come back to this fish. Joe Brooks, Al McLain, Lee Wulf. Of all the ones I've talked to who've had a chance to experience really nice salmon fishing, I don't know one who doesn't say, "Yeah, I have to agree. If I only had one fish to fish for, it would have to be the Atlantic salmon." I'll be a little closer to death when I know I can't fish for it anymore.

If you read the accounts of what salmon fishing was like in the past, you don't have to guess about the predicament it is in today. The stories tell of guys walking out into the rivers and spearing fifty fish at a clip, of natives catching so many they used them for fertilizer; but that was a long time ago. Indiscriminate fishing and the industrial pollution—sawmills, hydraulic dams, and so on—eventually choked the great rivers of New England so completely that the Atlantic salmon is now all but extinct in U.S. waters. Recent conservation programs have brought some of them back to certain rivers, but it is still a far cry from what it was.

In the rivers of eastern Canada the angler's limit was six a day when Roy Curtis started fishing forty years ago. Yet despite coordinated efforts to save the fish, the supply dwindled until now the limit is two a day and seven a week, and it's the devil to pay to get that. Besides all the other factors that have hammered at the fish the last few decades, the Danes discovered vast schools of salmon in the Davis Strait off Greenland in 1966.

The discovery solved some of the mysteries of where the fish go when they go to sea and how they make their return. The routes run along both the east and west coasts of Greenland, around Iceland, down the Davis Strait from Baffin Bay, and then split to the north of Labrador into the Hudson Bay and south along the Labrador Sea into Newfoundland, Nova Scotia, and New Brunswick.

But the Danes celebrated this find by pillaging. They devastated the salmon with drift and gill nets, some as much as ten miles long. Almost overnight the salmon rivers of Quebec, Newfoundland, and New Brunswick began experiencing diminished runs. The cries of outraged anglers got so loud the Danes eventually agreed to limit their netting. But high-seas fishing still takes an estimated 70 percent of the salmon caught every year, and native Greenlanders are still using inshore nets. Unfortunately now so are the commercial fishermen on the Miramichi. I suppose this eagerness to harvest the fish is a tribute to its popularity, but it hurts just the same. And once the salmon goes, who can replace it?

The Latin name is *Salmo salar*, "the leaper." The salmon is certainly that. Leaps as high as eleven feet have been reached by salmon making their way upstream to the spawning grounds. As a prize for anglers it has a rich history. Izaak Walton called it "the king of freshwater fish" in his classic fishing book, *The Compleat Angler*, in 1653. The kingdom stretches across the north Atlantic, from the Gulf of St. Lawrence to the Bay of Biscay.

But the Atlantic salmon I fish for, mainly on the Miramichi River in New Brunswick, is not necessarily the same as the Atlantic salmon caught in other places. The environments create shades of differences. In the Baltic, for example, the rivers are heavy and fast-flowing and the salmon are big, rugged, deep-water fish. The biggest salmon, as large as seventy pounds, are caught there, but the angler has to use heavy flies and heavy line on a rod so big and bulky he needs two hands to cast it. Spinning gear is used almost exclusively in those waters. All this makes for less than ideal salmon fishing.

Wherever you go you discover different techniques and feelings for this fish. And converts. When Franco came to power in Spain the salmon along that country's northern coast had just about had it. They had been speared and netted and abused in every way. But Franco was a fisherman and got interested, and being a dictator he was able to straighten out the problem with a few do-it-or-else edicts. The salmon came back to Spain and so did the angling for it. But, again, with spinning gear.

In the salmon rivers of North America, spinning isn't allowed any more. No netting, no gaffs. Nothing but fly-fishing. It is, of course, the ultimate way. But that doesn't mean there is no variety. Far from it. I

Of such as these are banquets made.

find subtle, intriguing differences from season to season, river to river, and pool to pool.

I have fished many of the great salmon rivers—the north shore of the St. Lawrence, the Restigouche, a few in Iceland—but my favorite remains the Miramichi, where I have a camp near Blackville. With its many tributaries, the Cains, the Dungarvon, the Renous, and more, the Miramichi system offers 400 miles of both public and private water and yielded a record 80,000 angled fish in 1966. At one time it produced more fish than all the other Canadian river systems combined. Jack Fenety of the Miramichi Salmon Association says that eleven different genetic strains of salmon are found in the Miramichi. They don't get as big as the salmon in the Restigouche, where thirty- and forty-pounders are not unusual, but you can fish them consistently in waders instead of in a canoe, and they are every bit as game.

The adult salmon has deep blue colorations on its back, and bright silvery sides and black cross-shaped markings on its head and body. Its underbelly is white and it has an adipose fin just in front of the tail fin. The adult male is called a hookbill for just that reason—it grows a hooked mouth that gets very pronounced in the spawning season. As a quarry the hookbill is generally a little more dogged, a little tougher than a hen, but not always. And they both vary physically from one period to another. For example, the early spring runs on the Mirami- chi produce a blockier fish, shorter, fatter, that is more eager to take a fly. But its mouth is tender. The fly is more inclined to tear loose.

The same is true with the fishing areas. The hot spots in some holes, the deeper, quieter places in the rivers where the fish tarry as they move upstream or down, seem to change from season to season and from high water to low water. A freshet can make a difference over- night. You have to be alert for changes. All the tricks and angles have to be tried and varied.

I remember fishing the Restigouche one year at a beautiful pool. The bigger salmon don't roll or jump as much, and I didn't see a thing for three days. All of a sudden there was a tremendous rolling boil, and I was about to cast out another foot and try him there when the fellow I was with said, "Just a minute now. Just reel *in* a foot. Reel in a foot and let it rest for twenty seconds before you cast again." I did. I got everything prepared and flipped the line out again. And caught a twenty-six-pounder.

The Tackle

There's no fish that's more fun to cast to and try things on than an Atlantic salmon, but the first rule in the book still applies: use adequate tackle. Casting 300 or 400 times a day, and I average that to land a single salmon, might make you think in terms of going to lighter gear, but you'll only cheat yourself; and you'll lose more fish and endanger the ones you do catch because it'll take longer playing them and they'll be slower to recover when released. Besides all that a fly zipping around erratically from too short a rod can stick in your ear or even your eye.

I use an eight-and-a-half-foot graphite rod of around three ounces, one that has good tip action and allows me to handle a No. 9 line and still cast long. When the wind is really bad, I might go to a nine-foot rod and still sacrifice a little distance. But more often than not eight-and-a-half to nine is adequate. The farther you can cast, the more water you can cover, even though most of the time you won't have to put it out more than sixty to eighty feet.

Retrieving line.

I like the luxury of being able to cast 90 to 100 feet if I have to, knowing I can still get distance when I'm facing a stiff wind. Day in, day out, my casts will average 75 to 80 feet. In exhibitions at sportsman's shows I cast over 100 feet and run into guys who can cast 130; but the true test of casting is on the river. In the wind. When you have to handle a lot of line and put a fly out in every imaginable condition.

You pretty much have to determine your own limits with the line you're using, but it's clear enough you shouldn't use anything you can't cast delicately. I use No. 8 to No. 9 shooting fly line, at least 150 yards of backing testing at thirty pounds. I use six- to eight-pound leader, ten with the bigger flies. I don't like a leader that's less than ten feet long or more then fourteen; mine is usually right in the middle at twelve feet. I feel I can cast precisely enough with that and still straighten it out into the wind.

I taper the nylon leader from a good stiff forty-pound butt down to thirty, twenty, fifteen, twelve, and then ten or eight, depending on whether I'm using six- or eight-pound tippet. I use as much tippet as I use butt in good conditions, and make all the pieces in between

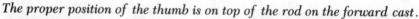

The proper position of the thumb is on top of the rod on the forward cast.

shorter than those two. Leader materials are getting better all the time, and even with an overhand knot they will test 80 percent. Years ago they wouldn't test 50 percent.

Roy Curtis, my guide and good friend, prefers a ten-pound tippet, and I don't think it hurts him. I don't think most salmon are leader-shy or fly-shy anyway; some of them have never seen either as they come upriver. So in that respect, 10-pound test is OK, but in low or clear water I prefer lighter. I have caught more than 200 salmon in a row without breaking one off with eight-pound, and on the occasion that I did it was late in the evening and my equipment was beaten down, the knots probably wearing out.

To tie the tapered leader, use blood knots, and every forty or fifty casts check your tippet. Knots deteriorate. They should be checked frequently, just as you check your leader or your fly. You're kidding yourself if you think a knot on a fly will hold its strength much past 100 casts. So as you work down the river, make it a point to check your knots every time you check your fly. (Do it especially when you're going through a known hot spot and aren't getting any action. It can be very exasperating to find out you have passed through a good area in a pool with a fouled-up fly.) The blood knot tests about 90 percent, and that means eight-pound test line will hold at around seven, which is enough.

I use No. 9 line because it'll handle any distance, any size fly—as large as a double four, as small as a double twelve. The only change I have to make is when I go to a heavier leader. I like the stiffer line. Fly lines should be much stiffer than most manufacturers make them. Limber line drags along the guides, creating friction and slowing itself down. I use Maxima fly leader—period.

A lot of guys say leader doesn't mean that much, but if you don't have proper tapering to the right size fly, you'll be making little casting errors all the time. The leader has to complement the fly to make it ride right. If you use too light a leader for the size of the fly, three things can happen, all bad: one, you can break the fish off, two, you can wear down the knot so you won't be able to apply any tension to it, or three, you will be unable to straighten the fly out. It'll be too heavy for the tippet.

With eight-pound test I can tie my flies to small hooks, a double No. 6 or a single No. 8. If I use bigger flies, I go to ten-pound test. When the water's up, I use a little bigger fly, with a double six or even a double four.

I tie almost all my flies to softer wired regular steel hooks, as opposed to forged hooks that I think are too hard to offset. Occasionally a soft hook will straighten out a little under pressure but not as much as you'd think. I use a Mustadd 3399 single and English doubles.

If you're using twelve-pound leader, you'll have to have even bigger flies. The leader-to-fly ratio of line thickness figures something like this: the diameter of twelve-pound test line is $\frac{1}{13,000}$ of an inch; ten-pound test line is $\frac{1}{12,000}$; eight-pound is $\frac{1}{10,500}$ to $\frac{1}{11,000}$; and so forth. You graduate down to achieve continual flow of momentum, whatever it takes to lightly turn over the fly at the farthest point of the cast and make the fly swim properly. If your fly is too heavy for the tippet, it won't turn over as nicely. This, of course, applies to all fly-fishing.

If you're having trouble with the wind, don't be reluctant to change your leader. When you have a favorable wind, you might lengthen both leader and tippet; it will sink better. When you're into a strong wind, you might want to shorten your leader. Don't be afraid to make changes to suit your own style and the conditions and to take into account peculiarities in the equipment itself. Often one fly line will cast differently than another even when it tests the same. There is a tolerance of twenty to thirty grains in each weight category, and differences occur.

One other knot that you should experiment with, one that will help make your swim suit the water, is called a Portland hitch or a riffle hitch. Actually all it is is a half hitch tied around the head of the fly so that it gently tugs the fly to the side of the river you're fishing. If, for example, you're on the right-hand bank, you throw the half hitch behind the right side of the fly's head. I usually tie a second hitch to secure it better.

The knot makes the fly riffle as it cuts through the water. Makes it look a little like a tiny mouse swimming. I don't use the riffle all that much. I haven't found it that productive, but it's fun to try when the water's slick and has good movement. And when nothing else is working. The first time I caught a salmon on a riffle hitch was an accident. I'd thrown the hitch into the leader while casting and saw it only when I took the fish off.

Which brings us to the flies themselves, the *pièce de résistance*. Half the thrill of salmon fishing for me is tying my own flies. That totals about 400 or 500 thrills a year. Fortunately most of the better salmon flies, especially those used on the Miramichi, are very simple flies that take no more than ten minutes to tie. But they can give you as much pride and satisfaction as the complicated ones, because you can concentrate more on making them a little neater, a little better shaped, a little better lacquered, and they are just as effective. Unfortunately most fly tiers don't take that extra trouble.

There are hundreds of varieties of salmon flies. Most of them have hair wings and provocative names, Silver Rat, Rusty Ray, Dusty Miller, Jock Scott, and so forth. Most of them have hackles made of the saddle feathers and neck feathers of a goose or a duck, or an exotic bird from Africa or the Orient, wound around the shank of the hook to flare out. Out of 100 salmon flies, 99 are wet flies, and the secret I've learned is that the smaller flies are the best. But the patterns and size vary with the conditions of the water. The heavier and dirtier the water, the bigger and brighter the flies. Quite often in moderate to low water, in a slow moving pool, I use a dry fly. The best for me is the Bomber, a big, deer-haired bug that floats especially well.

A deadly foursome: double-twelves on a kitchen match.

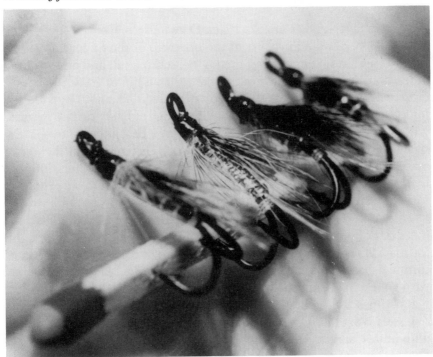

Most flies on the Miramichi are simple designs, but must be tied well to be effective.

My two favorite flies are the Black Does and the Conrad. The Black Does is a dark-bodied fly, sort of the opposite of the Silver Gray. The Black Does has silver tinsel on the tag behind the tail and on the curve of the hook, yellow floss in front of that, then a tail of golden pheasant crest. The body is black floss ribbed with silver. The hackle, from the middle of the fly forward, is black, with wings of black turkey married with strands of red, yellow, and blue swan. The fibers between the strands are combed and rubbed together. It has macaw in it, bronze mallard, jungle cock eyes, altogether twenty or twenty-five different feathers. Using all these ingredients makes the Black Does a lot of fun to tie, but it is still basically a simple fly.

The Conrad is the most popular on the Miramichi. A year-round fly, it is a dark fly with gantrin, a synthetic material that reflects the light, for sparkle, a golden pheasant tail, gold wire, a gold tag, and the most distinguishable part, a gantrin green butt. It has a black body, ribbed with gold wire, bear-hair wings, and a very sparsely tied black hackle. I sometimes add golden jungle cock eyes to brighten it up even more.

I use a No. 6 hook, a No. 8, or even a double eight or ten with light wire on a Conrad. Salmon hooks will range from a double twelve to double two, and single eights to single threes, but more and more salmon anglers are going to smaller hooks. A No. 6 or No. 8 is all you need if everything else is right. My experience is that salmon prefer small hooks, but hook selection depends on the water conditions—a No. 4, say, at the mouth of the river where the water is heavier, a No. 8 in clearer, lighter water.

The best thing about small hooks is that a wary fish that has gotten skittish from having so many big flies thrown at him might find them more appetizing. Too, a small single hook makes it easier to release a fish. All you have to do is give it a little nip. Off goes the fish, unharmed.

When the water is up, I use a bigger hook, a double six or a double four and, more than likely, flashier flies, like the Dusty Miller or the Silver Cassaboom. The Butterfly is a showy fly with white wings that spread out and have a scissors action and a peacock body and brown hackle. You always need a showy fly in the spring when the water's high and moving hard, something to excite the salmon's interest as he moves. When the summer comes and there's less rain and run-off from the woods, you go to your small flies with lighter, finer leaders.

I like turned-down eyes for wet flies and up for dry. The former forces the fly to ride a little deeper in the water; the latter helps keep it riding the surface.

If you haven't gotten into tying your own flies, of course you can just buy them. If you don't care to ever get involved tying them, I'd advise you never to tie the first one.

The Conditions

As long as I am near a salmon river, no matter what the conditions, rain or shine, hot weather or cold, high water or low, in sickness or in health, the day is not likely to go by without me fishing. I am as nuts about it in a cold, pouring rain as I am in bright sunshine. I love it that much. But there are better times than others, and if your opportunity to fish is limited, you need to know them to pick your shots.

The early spring is the time when the so-called black salmon come downriver. They have been iced in all winter, eating nothing, and they come down at 60 to 75 percent of their original body weight, weakened, gaunt, and so ugly the natives call them slinks. Because they are voracious eaters, black salmon get some attention from anglers, but I find them uninteresting and very poor eating, so I don't bother. They clear out of the river in two or three weeks anyway.

The salmon to fish for are the ones going upstream, and the first of those, the spring-run salmon, start in May. These fish are bright, fat, and eager. Prime salmon. I use bigger flies on them because the water is usually deeper and maybe a little discolored from the spring runoffs. Also, spring salmon have tender mouths. You have to be careful or your fly will tear loose. A larger fly helps you stay with them better.

These early-run salmon were originally spawned far upriver and are in a big hurry getting back there to spawn again. They're mostly hens from nine to twenty pounds, averaging around twelve. Adult salmon. The runs get bigger in number into June. Then comes the summer-run salmon, starting in July, when the water is clearer. There is a heavy complement of grilse (salmon that have come back to their spawning river after only one year at sea and now weigh around four pounds) among the full size salmon. July is a grilse month. Your chances of getting fish in July are excellent.

Meanwhile the river rises and falls with the amount of summer rainfall but gradually gets lower and lower. The height of the water is a constant fishing factor. From the bigger, heavier flies I use when the water is up, I switch to smaller flies when by August the water is at its lowest and clearest and least active.

August can bring the worst conditions for catching fish. The water is low, slow, and hot, with less oxygen. Strange things are liable to happen. The fish take different bugs and dry flies. They take fouled-up lures. It can be a confusing time for the angler who thinks he knows the patterns. Making it worse in recent years has been the clear cutting of adjoining forests. With no trees to stop them, the drain-offs into the rivers have been much hotter and dirtier. In August the fish don't lay in the same pools they did in June or July, or they lay lower in them. The pools in the lower parts of the river are more active then because there is less water farther up. In August you hope for freshets, the small rainstorms that bring in cool water and entice the fish up from the bay. You fish early in the morning and late in the evening.

My feeling is that any time the water gets above 70 or 72 degrees you might as well stay home. The fish are less lively, and adult salmon are reluctant to come upriver. You seldom see a salmon when the water temperature exceeds 65 degrees. I've caught grilse at 78 degrees, but that's rare. The salmon won't take the fly on the swing. They tend to take it at the very end when the fly is moving at its slowest. Or they take in slow water, which indicates they aren't that eager to move.

All in all I think the ideal water temperature on the Miramichi is around 55 degrees. For fish in the more northern rivers the temperature would have to be a little cooler. But at 55 degrees, the Miramichi's salmon are lively and fast. They move good. They take the fly on the swing and come up on it eagerly.

September brings the late-run, the fall-run, salmon, and conditions improve immensely. You generally get your biggest fish in September. They come into the river fully developed, ready and ripe to spawn. They are a distinctly different color, and the hookbills among them have much more pronounced hooks. They are also slower moving. They tend to mooch along the river. The water is usually down, and they don't make those surging runs to the head of the river the way the earlier fish do.

But the water is also colder, and the fall fish are much more showy. They roll, they jump. They stay in the pools better. They are liable to hang around one spot all day and not make a move to go upriver. All this makes the fishing more exciting in the fall. You spot a fish and you say to yourself, "All right, I know you're there, I'll be back." You might make passes at him five times without getting a roll. Then, maybe late in the afternoon, he begins to get a little nervous, and he gets ready to pull out—and boom, you're there with a fly.

Because they tarry like that, late-run salmon are so bombarded by flies that they get very wary, but that of course just makes it more challenging. And because there are more salmon than grilse in this run and the fish don't go as far upriver, your chances for a big one are good.

I like the water during the build to the moon. The tides get higher and higher, and the fish move in that water all night and into mid-morning. The time to fish them is from around eight A.M. to five P.M., while they're holding in the pools. I'm not as keen about a completely full moon. They don't perform as well then.

The water to look for has a good flow but is not too deep. Salmon lay on the bottom when they're not moving, and if you're casting into a pool that is ten feet deep and they have to come up eight feet or so to get to the fly, they probably won't bother. They'd rather come three or four or even two feet.

Look for current through a gravelly or rocky bottom. That indicates the water has moved through and cleaned out the sand and mud. Mud bottoms indicate slower water, and you aren't as likely to catch fish there. Your fly won't work as well, and it will swing more slowly, which means you will have to wait longer between casts. You waste a lot of time in slow water. The fish can take all the time they want making up their minds about a fly.

The good runs are all gravel and rock bottomed. Fish lay below the bars in the shallow, gravelly places three to six feet deep, depending on the height of the water. The ideal salmon pool has a deeper hole at the lower end for the salmon to slip into for coolness and protection. This is usually the place to try dry flies. The faster the water the more apt you are to get one on in shallow water; the deeper water will be slower, without as much current. When the water is flowing good, there is more oxygen in it. That makes the fish livelier, and a livelier fish is a more eager taker.

There are times, of course, when you won't have a choice. In late July and early August, for example, if there hasn't been any rain, you may be facing dead water all the time and warmer water, which is less oxygenated. You learn to be a little more patient and to compensate by speeding up the fly, helping it along by pulling it smoothly through the arc of the swing, with a little greater angle across, or by switching to a dry fly.

If I had my druthers, I'd say the ideal speed of the water would be five to ten miles an hour, and the proper depth of the pools to fish in, three to six feet. Ideally you would fish that pool in waders rather than in a canoe. In waders you can cover the water with more mobility and won't be stopping to fool with an anchor.

To know which pools are high-water pools and which are better in low water, you have to pay attention to the fish's movement. In some pools when it's low, the fish stay right there, but if the water rises two feet, they go through without even slowing up.

My preference is high water over low any day, because when the water's high, the fish come. And if I had a choice, I'd pick the beginning of a rise, because the fish will take before the water is too discolored. When it gets discolored, it's a signal for them to move on. By the same token a few days after a freshet can be productive, too. When the surge of the cooler water reaches the fish waiting in the bay, it'll make them move; the fishing gets active again as the water drops upriver.

The Angling

For this fish a proper and thorough introduction is necessary. It is only right that guides are required on the salmon rivers of eastern Canada. There are more factors to Atlantic salmon fishing than you can count, and it pays to have a guide who knows every pool in his area of the river, good and bad. A guide who knows water conditions, who can anticipate when fish are coming in, who knows the areas where it is treacherous to wade and the rocks and holes to cast to, and as important as anything else, who knows the private water from the public and can keep you from infringing on someone else's pool.

The joy of fishing for Atlantic salmon is for me directly related to the joy of casting. I may get tired casting, but I never get tired *of* casting. For Atlantic salmon the pleasure is accentuated by a constant anticipation. You're right there, in beautiful settings, fishing close. Seeing fish roll. Seeing them jump. Seeing them move in the water.

By contrast, take a redfish. Your cast for a redfish puts you out maybe 100 yards, sometimes with a fish-finder rig. The bait goes out, and you leave it there, or you crank it back and do it again. The process takes forever, and you never see anything until a fish hits.

For salmon I am on the river at eight A.M. and break around noon, then go back after an early supper and fish until dusk. I figured it out once that I average around 3 casts a minute, 300 to 400 casts a day. That's more than half a million casts since my first trip to the Miramichi over thirty years ago. And I never get tired of it.

The fundamentals of salmon fishing are no big secret, but you should review them nevertheless. You always cast cross-river, at anywhere from a forty-five- to a fifty-five-degree angle against the direction of the current, depending on the speed of the water and the lies, the places salmon hold in. That way your fly swings around naturally and rides an arc with the flow. If you cast straight downriver, there is no arc, no swing, no movement.

I cast right-handed. When I get on the river, I establish how much line I intend to cast. I usually start with a little less than maximum and build up, but the average cast for me will almost always be in the neighborhood of seventy-five to eighty feet. I get that much line out. When it's out, and the fly has completed the swing and is straight downstream, I slowly lift the rod to about a forty-five-degree angle. This gives me a cushion in case a fish comes up from behind and takes the fly. If he does, I can easily drop the rod tip to him. With that little flex in the rod he won't be able to hit a straight line.

Now the elements of the cast. I start retrieving line from downstream. I strip in six times, about four feet a strip. I strip once or twice on the water and four or five times in my hand, with the line still downstream. Then I pick the line up, and if I'm on the right-hand side of the river, I flick it behind me to the right, fifteen or twenty degrees, then cast it out onto the river fifteen or twenty degrees to my left. That gives me about fifty feet of line out, including leader and forward taper. Then I flick it back with a double haul and shoot about twenty-five more feet at that forty-five-degree angle from the direction of the current.

As soon as I throw the line out, I straighten it by stripping it tight. I don't wait for the current to straighten it because by then I will have lost two to four feet of effective swimming of the fly. I want it as straight as possible as quickly as possible, so that it will swim correctly. Salmon are most likely to take the fly when it is swimming properly.

Always work with the elements. If the wind is behind you, make a higher forward cast to let it help carry the fly. When you have to cast into the wind, *push* your wrist forward to build momentum and keep the line low. Don't break your wrist until your arm is fully extended. Into the wind you will want to double haul.

On the double haul, as I lift the rod to start my back cast, I take my left hand and pull the line sharply down from the first guide. This loads the rod and makes for a more positive back cast. As the line goes behind me, I follow it up with my left hand, again to the first guide of the rod. At the extent of the back cast, I start my forward motion as a high push, at about a twenty- to twenty-five-degree angle, and with my left hand, again pull down on the line, reloading the rod. Then I shoot it all out.

The back cast is always lower than the forward cast, on about the same plane but opposite to that twenty to twenty-five degrees. This is under ideal conditions. When I cast into the wind, I make my forward cast at a lower angle, approximately ten degrees off the water. In either case, however, the double haul puts more load on the rod and speeds up the line. And it certainly allows you to cast more efficiently into the wind.

Now, when the fly hits, your arm should be fully extended, with the wrist straight. At that point your first move is a slight pull on the line to tighten and straighten it out. You want the fly to start swimming properly as soon as possible, because you might get lucky with that first cast and throw right on a fish.

The drift of a fly has a simple purpose—to make the fly swim naturally. You don't want the leader to belly out ahead of the fly. That usually happens when you cast too much cross-stream. You can cast cross-stream and mend the belly upstream two or three times, but that's only a correction. I'd prefer to cast at the proper angle for the speed of the water and adjust to that speed. Sometimes you might throw straight across when you see a fish roll, but for that kind of cast I'd be more inclined to use a bomber, a dry fly, and try to get a free drift—just let it drag on around.

Ideally the fly should pass cross-stream to the salmon you're after, so that he sees the whole side of the fly. He might take it almost head-on, but it's better if he sees it as it flattens out and starts to move away from him. That's the time he is most likely to come to the fly from his lie.

If I'm casting from the right side of the river and the fly swings around to his right and starts to swing by, he'll meet the fly and turn with it to the right, which means he'll take it in the left side of his jaw. That's important to remember. Salmon almost always hit the fly on the side of their mouths as they turn toward the middle of the stream.

In all water the "swing is the thing," the right speed of the fly as it swings through the arc. In slack water you may need to encourage the lure to swim faster. More skill is needed then because the line will not allow the fly to swim as well. You help it along by putting a little more tension on the tip of the rod, in effect, pulling it through the water.

I saw a long-time Miramichi regular named Max Gillespie do that years ago. He gave his fly more tension by stripping in ever so slightly to increase the speed in slack water. At the end of the swing he gave it a little extra pull to make it go faster. I remember noticing it because he was the only one of about fifteen anglers who caught a fish that day. And I've been using that same trick ever since. The extra speed, that little extra life, excites the fish. It was brought home even clearer to me a few years later. I'd made my "last cast of the day," pulling the fly through the last third of the arc, inadvertently speeding it up as I was moving out of the water, when a salmon hit. A twelve-pounder.

You must remember, however, that you never speed up a fly to the point that it is not compatible with the speed of the current. You don't, for example, make a fly look like it's in a ten-mile current when the current is moving only three miles an hour; but in gauging it, if you find the fly needs that extra help to make it speed up and swing around more enticingly, just put that extra tension on the tip of your rod.

To slow down the swim of the fly, as you might want to do in faster water, you simply use a little less angle on your cross-stream cast. You can decrease the bend of the line from the rod tip, too. In real fast water or when you see something that makes you think slowing the swim will raise a fish, mend the line, which is to say, throw another loop cross-stream so that the fly will pause and straighten out. That eases the tension from rod tip to fly and straightens the line at the same time. The straighter the line, the less speed of the fly. The more loop, the more speed. You can get about the same results with tension on the tip—more tension, more speed, for example.

When the water is extra fast, you don't want to accentuate the speed, so you put less angle between your rod tip as the fly progresses in its arc. I prefer that to mending the line, because it's more natural. It is more important the fly swim naturally.

You learn and adjust as you go, and in salmon fishing you go slowly. You work downstream, usually in a long line of fellow anglers, with just enough room all around to cast. Watch the other anglers—you can always learn. You "fish by the foot," covering water. You cast at that forty-five-degree angle, let the lure swim around until it's straight off your rod, wait a few moments, then take a step or two downriver, and do it again. Be careful of your footing. A slip on the downside of a rock and you'll have your waders full of icy water, and unless you carry extra clothes as I do, a damp day ahead. Wade sideways to the current so that most of your weight is on your back foot as you step.

You keep working down through the pool, casting, letting the fly swing around, waiting, casting again, taking another step. Cast, wait, and so forth.

If you roll a fish, don't move. Freeze right there. Pull in—don't reel—and try it again. If he doesn't take, check your fly. Wait. Let him return to his lie. (If it's before nine or ten A.M., you might quickly try another cast, because he could be moving then, but otherwise you wait.) Record where you are and where you think the fish is by noting landmarks, a rock there, a birch tree there. Don't change the length of the line you've got out, but take it in and wait. Some guys go up on shore and light a pipe before they cast again just so they can let the fish settle down. I don't.

Now if you cast and he still doesn't take, you might decide it's time to make changes—in the technique, in the lure. Try another fly. Change the arc of the swing, usually by taking a step in or out. The angle on a salmon is very important. The more experienced you are, the more you will know about casting angles on a fish. From the salmon's standpoint the fly is most exciting at the moment near the end of the swing when it is gaining speed. Ideally you would like the fly to pass in front of the fish at that point. That little extra speed gives the illusion of a fly trying to get away. The "happy zone" of the swing is that last fifteen to twenty degrees to the point where the line finally straightens out.

Much of the pleasure in salmon fishing is in learning enough to profit from your mistakes—adjusting to the conditions, trying new things. You get a fish to come up, a nice one rolls, and either the fly wasn't right, or something changes his mind, and you miss him. After you've given him every chance to take from the spot and angle you're casting, you go through the rituals: shorten the cast by moving your position upriver or down, in or out . . . change the angle of the cast . . . speed up the drift of the fly, or mend it and slow it down . . . put a bigger belly in the line . . . let the fly sink a little deeper . . . and so on.

You try any or all of those things when you're onto a fish, and it's all fun. The closest-to-heaven feeling for a salmon fisherman occurs during those times when he knows a fish is there and he's trying to find the combination.

When you know he's there, you've given him every opportunity, and he still hasn't taken, bring the fly in and check it out, change the fly, check the knots. In doing that, you are also giving the fish a chance to go back to where he was resting, to settle down and not dash out of the area. It's very important to do this on a holding fish. If you're in a line of anglers, you might have to move on, but if you've marked the spot and remembered what you've tried, you can pick up where you left off the next time through.

All the moves you make are to one purpose: to get the fly over the desired spot in the most advantageous angle. Moving in or out might not be any help at all if the fish has rolled way out in the middle of the stream, out where the current is swifter. You might want to move upriver then, to an easier, more shallow angle. But the point is that there are no hard and fast rules; you have to try everything.

You only learn to read the fish, their rolls and rolling turns and jumps, by seeing them in action and recognizing the differences. You will learn to tell almost instinctively if a fish is moving fast or slow, just by a roll, or if he's on an elevator to and from his holding place. The angler who doesn't pay attention will always be a novice. He'll see a fish roll, and he'll miss the fish's intentions. He'll have no idea of the reason because he won't know why it happened, because of his fly or in spite of it.

I don't say you have to try to think like a salmon, but they are predictable in ways that you can learn. Their instincts bring them back along predictable paths. I got a twenty-pounder one day on the Cains River, and the very next day at the very same rock I got another twenty-pounder. Both were hens, and they looked almost identical. I kept the first one, so I know they were different, but I also got a picture of each one, taken separately, and in the pictures I had different shirts on. I have no doubt in my mind those two fish were spawned together, hatched together, went to sea together, came back together, and wound up the same size in the same place—on instinct.

There are, of course, no guarantees that anything will work. I had a fish come after my fly five times once at Swinging Bridge on the Mira-

From that first flashing dimple on the water to the final lift-out, there is nothing more satisfying than a salmon catch.

155

michi. He rolled and rolled again, right at the fly, and never took it. The salmon never completely showed himself. I tried everything— four to five different flies, changing the angle of my casts, everything. And it was no use.

Another time I was using a dry fly, and I had what I thought was a grilse come up on it five times, putting his nose in the fly. The whole thing was happening no more than eight or ten feet away. He finally took it and turned out to be a fourteen-pound hookbill.

Despite all that, this is a fish that you always feel confident about. You always think you'll come up with some technique, some fly that will get him, that it'll be this cast with this fly. You get that feeling when you've learned enough to know what's going on, and it never leaves you.

When you've hooked a salmon, there isn't that great explosion you get with a tarpon or the slow pull and then the mad dash of the bone- fish. It's actually like nothing you experience anywhere else in angling. Sometimes, of course, a salmon will do those little nagging numbers— peck at it, rake it with his mouth—but generally he comes up to it with an unmistakable roll. Smooth, positive, beautiful—authoritative without being too eager, as if he knows exactly what he's doing.

The exception would be in the summertime, when the water's warm and the fish aren't as enthusiastic rolling on a fly. Then you have to be ready to set the hook not according to what you see but by what you feel. And what you feel is the weight of the fish, that distinguish- ing pull. You strike then.

Under no circumstances do you ever try to get too big with a salmon. In fact you should have very little drag on your reel at all, less than half a pound, just enough to keep the line from spinning off the reel. There are times in the season when you have to be more careful than others, of course. As I said, the spring run produces fish with softer mouths that are more susceptible to having a hook tear out. The fall run produces tougher fish. You don't have to be quite as cautious with them.

You treat a salmon strike delicately. Not gently, or tenderly, but delicately, as if it were something that could explode. I've been doing that since the first time I fished for salmon, when Julian Crandall, the president of Ashawa Line, bet me I'd break off the first two I hooked. I was extra careful that day. It paid off, and I've been careful ever since.

But also remember that *Salmo salar* is a leaper, a jumping fish. Come up delicately but positively, and keep your rod up. If you're in fast water, and the fly is really swinging, and he hits in the middle of the swing, that's all you will have to do, and he'll be hooked. In slow water you might have to goose it a little, be more positive with your strike. Again, however, don't set the hook until you feel the weight of the salmon, then come up smoothly. The exception would be in that really slow-moving pool, when the fish takes a fly that is barely moving. Strike immediately then.

Unfortunately you can't get experience out of a book, and much of what you do under various circumstances will depend on how much you've learned—after you've learned to cast and after you've learned a little about the fish. You learn, for example, from the fly line, the way it swings, the speed it travels. You learn from the roll of a fish. You should be able to tell instantly what it is doing by the way it rolls, whether it is waving at you and moving on, see you later, or is holding. You get a big boil, and it looks like the salmon has stopped at the last second from taking the fly: chances are he will be holding, laying up in the pool; he just couldn't decide.

As soon as you've got him hooked and as much under control as you can manage while he goes through those first wild salmon antics—jumping, running, jumping again—you begin to ease your way toward the shore. Play him from there, from shallow water, so that you can make whatever move is necessary, up or down the river.

You should know instinctively to drop the tip when the salmon jumps, to give him the slack he needs to keep the line from breaking, then to come right back up on him. As I said, you never get too big. Don't think in terms of turning him; think in terms of pressuring him. Let him run, but keep after him.

If he's a really hot fish, he's liable to go anywhere, upriver or down, in or out. Move with him so that you can fight him from the side rather than from upstream. When he's moving cross-stream or downstream, try to put pressure on the upriver side of him. That's a form of turning, but it's a little more subtle. The main thing is to be cross-stream or down-stream as you play him.

When you're near the point of netting him, don't hold your rod too high. Keep it more perpendicular to his body to move him toward shore. Don't lift him. Flex the tip low to the drag and pull the hook back toward you. Try to swim him into the net. Your guide will take care of the netting, but if you're going to keep the fish, you can just as well bring him right onto the rocks in the shallow water.

Always remember, however, that this is a wonderful, valuable fish. If you aren't absolutely sure you want to keep him, treat him as tenderly as you can on the release. Handle him as if he were an infant.

Don't do anything to hurt him. If you've been using double hooks and have trouble getting them out, quit using them. Give the fish a chance.

After fishing for salmon so long, I've learned to adjust in many ways. Hooks, for example. I started off using nothing but single hooks and lost a lot of fish. I switched to doubles and did better. I got more fish per strike with doubles than with singles, but another factor was at work, a disadvantage that eventually got me back to using singles for good. Double hooks foul up more easily on the leader. If you pass over a hot spot with a fouled-up fly, nothing is likely to happen.

Singles are also easier to cast. Whereas you may get more fish per strike with a double, I think more fish rise to a single hook. It adds up this way: with a single, you get fewer fouled-up flies, you cast better, you release quicker and more safely. A lot of anglers are coming to that conclusion. Some of them feel doubles ought to be outlawed because they allow you to jig a fish. I'm not so sure about that, but I do feel a lot better all around when I catch a salmon on a single hook.

A couple of more thoughts, then I'm done. Some anglers never use a dry fly, and I don't use them very often, but if you don't use dry flies occasionally, you're missing a lot of fun, and you're not a complete salmon fisherman. The best time, I've found, for dry flies is after mid-morning, when the fish are holding.

Incidentally the prevailing wind is always best, but that applies to all fishing. The wind is only a factor in salmon fishing in relation to how tough it is to cast. When it's in your face, you can afford to make a little longer back cast, because the wind is helping you. The more weight you can put forward under control, the farther that cast will go into the wind.

Under all conditions be appreciative of the Atlantic salmon. It's the greatest fish that swims, and you are privileged when you have had a chance to fish for him.

I'll never forget one rainy, cold day on the Renous River. I was going to a spot that took me through the yard of a New Brunswick native. Out of the unpainted, dilapidated house came a little boy of about twelve, wearing tattered tennis shoes and not nearly enough clothes to keep him warm. He escorted me to the river. I felt so bad for him that I said if he showed me the hot spots, I'd give him the first fish I caught.

It wasn't long afterward that I hooked a nice salmon, about ten to twelve pounds, but it was a hen. A hen that size will lay seven to eight thousand eggs when it gets upstream. It's an important fish to everybody.

A hookbill Ted took in front of his cabin in low water in the early 1960's.

The kid saw me catch it, and as I was about to release it, he came over and I told him what the potential of that hen was. How it would be a shame to keep it.

"Yeah," he said. "That's right. We oughta let this fish go."

Unfortunately I never saw the boy again. But he knew about Atlantic salmon, all right.

MY CROWD

FEUERBACH and HANSEN
BRIELLE, N.J.

What follows is the evidence of
a man's love of fishing, a lifetime of memories after having
fished for just about everything an angler could hope to
fish for. Upper right: Two
Baseball Hall-of-Famers after
a memorable day off Brielle,
N.J. The young Jimmy Foxx
(far right, standing) and the
even younger Ted Williams
(second from right, kneeling)
played havoc with a school
of bluefin tuna the day after a
Red Sox game in Philadelphia.
At left: Ted's first "big" fish—
a 397-pound tuna caught in
1941.

163

Examining a smallmouth bass with Dr. Tom Shortell, the orthopedic surgeon who helped Ted recover from an elbow injury in 1950.

164

Ray P. Holland first interested Williams in Florida with his stories about the fighting ability of the snook.

A simple pattern for tarpon.

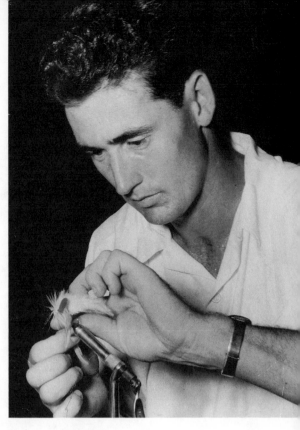

Exaggerating a catch for Jim Thorpe, "the greatest athlete who ever lived."

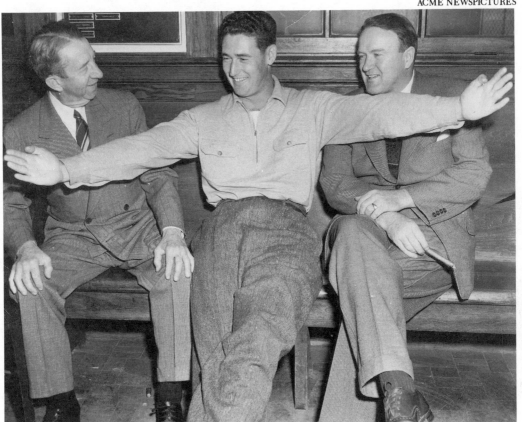

An even greater exaggeration for the Red Sox' Eddie Collins (left) and Joe Cronin after signing his contract.

A speckled trout on Fish Lake in Maine.

168

Smallmouth bass, caught with Lloyd Clarke in Maine.

A 22-pound muskie, the biggest Ted ever caught.

Fishing the city reservoir outside Boston.

Watching the marlin get "branded."

When Ted landed this 1,235-pound black marlin at Cabo Blanco, Peru, in 1954, it was the eighth largest ever caught. His close friend Julian Crandall (left) of Ashaway Fishing Lines landed an 800-pounder the same trip.

171

Ted often appeared with Jack Sharkey, the former heavyweight champion, at sportsmen's shows.

With fishing buddy Frank Tiernan and another big permit.

173

A 22-pound permit.

Comparing spinning- and fly-tackle catches with Buffalo Bob Smith of the Howdy Doody show.

WM. J. McCARTHY, JR.

WM. J. McCARTHY, JR.

WM. J. McCARTHY, JR.

"Fishing" at a sportsmen's show. With 30-pound-test line, Ted and his opponent battle human swimmers.

A lesson, and a prize, for son John Henry on his first fishing trip.

Daughter Claudia has just begun to fish, but clearly enjoys it.

Daughter Bobby Jo is a mother herself now, but she was an eager bonefisherwoman as a youngster.

Heading out to sea with the always-eager John Henry.

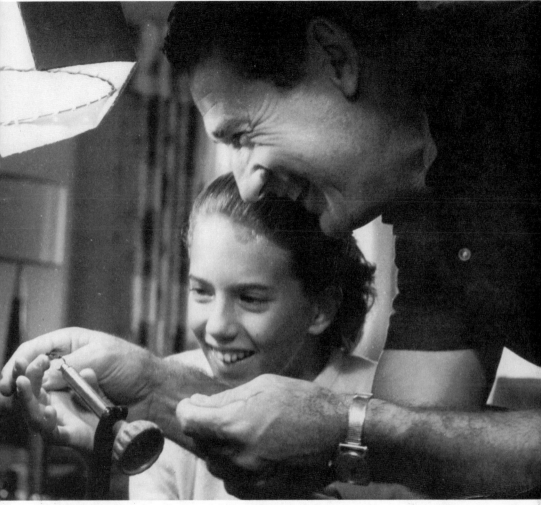

Bobby Jo watches her dad tie a fly.

On a first-time trip to New Zealand, Ted bagged three deer, four rainbow trout, and a 500-pound thresher shark—all within ten hours.

Admiring Stu Apte's bonefish on the lower Florida Keys.

Bandleader Benny Goodman also found bonefish a hot number.

Trout fishing at Grandfather's Mountain, N.C.

Playing a big fish with a New Zealand reel.

Time out for lunch with Cecil Keith.

Ted's first big sailfish.

189

ABOUT THE AUTHORS

TED WILLIAMS

No fan need be told who Ted Williams was when baseball was his sport. The last of the .400 hitters, American League batting champion six times, home run champion four times, and the holder of several other major league records, he is regarded by many as the greatest hitter who ever lived and was named to the Baseball Hall of Fame in 1966. His two previous books (also written with John Underwood), *My Turn at Bat* and *The Science of Hitting,* are baseball classics.

In more recent years he has established a comparable reputation as this country's outstanding fisherman, and this is his first book on that topic. It too is destined to be a sports classic.

JOHN UNDERWOOD

John Underwood is a senior writer for *Sports Illustrated,* and his work for that magazine, and earlier for the *Miami Herald* and *Miami News,* has won awards. In addition to his collaboration with Ted Williams he has several other sports books to his credit, including *Bear, When in Doubt, Fire the Manager,* and *The Death of an American Game.* He attended the University of Miami and makes his home in that city, along with his wife and four children.